Favorite Recipes of

of

The Lady & Her Friends

Paula H. Deen
The Lady & Sons Restaurant
102 West Congress Street
Savannah, GA 31401

Dedication

The most devoted supporters and confidants of my adult
life have been my Aunt Peggy and Uncle George Ort.
It is to Aunt Peggy and in fond memory of my Uncle George
that this work is most affectionately dedicated.

[1997]

Paula Deen Ventures
2391 Downing Ave.
PDV Thunderbolt, GA 31404

2017 edition copyright © by Paula H. Deen

Library of Congress Cataloging-in-Publication data is available.

ISBN 978-1-943016082

22 21 20 19 18 17   10 9 8 7 6 5 4 3 2 1

TWENTY YEARS LATER

After I opened the restaurant The Lady & Sons, my goal was to write a cookbook. I remember pouring all of my recipes out of a brown paper sack—recipes that included ones I inherited from my mother. Seeing Momma's handwriting and remembering all the delicious meals she cooked up made me smile. I asked family, friends, and customers to submit recipes for my little book; and to show that cooking was fun, I asked Geri Jacobs to illustrate a few stories I shared with her.

For this twentieth-anniversary edition, I wanted to publish the book exactly like the original 5,000 copies printed in 1997. But when I wrote this book, I just assumed everyone had the same kitchen knowledge I had. Since then, I've learned a lot about writing cookbooks, so I changed a few things. I can now assure you that all recipes have been tested—but I can't say the same for the 1997 edition! And my recipes were not always clear: for example, "1 cup onions" should have been "1 cup *chopped onion*." Typos have been fixed—and there were a few. I have also changed all margarine references to butter. Let me take this opportunity to share that over the past years so much has been written touting the benefits of butter over margarine. So butter is best! Also, while reading through all of these recipes and remembering all of my friends, I could not help but add new comments.

This edition matches the original book's design. But I wanted to re-create the cover showing how the Lady & Sons staff has grown. The original cover photograph included Jamie, Bobby, Aunt Peggy, myself, and our 19 employees. The new photo includes only a small portion of the current 216 employees; however, I am proud to say that a few of the faces in both photos are the same. As for the back cover, Jamie, Bobby, and I had fun re-creating the original back cover photo, right down to the placement of our hands.

During the filming of *Midnight in the Garden of Good and Evil* in Savannah, a New York City publisher came into The Lady & Sons and bought a copy of my little cookbook, and that is the day our lives changed. The publisher purchased *Favorite Recipes of The Lady & Her Friends* to publish as *The Lady & Sons Savannah Country Cookbook*, and it became a best-seller. But during all these years, I had never realized that 150 recipes had been dropped and had never been published. I am so excited to publish a complete edition of my very first cookbook.

Paula H. Deen

2017

Acknowledgements

A special *"Thank you"* to all those who have so generously contributed their cherished Heirloom Recipes toward the success of this cookbook. We also thank those from whom we have begged, borrowed, or perhaps stolen! We have used all the recipes this book could accommodate, without duplication. If your favorite is missing, please forgive us.

We acknowledge and appreciate the expert cooks who have shared their culinary secrets for publication herein. We have reviewed all the recipes; however, they have not necessarily been individually tested in our kitchens.

Our sincere thanks to Ms. Geri Jacobs for contributing her artistic hand lettering and graphic designs to the creation of the caricatures. Her expertise has added to the fun and joy of this project.

We appreciate the superb assistance of Dr. Barbara Bart of Savannah State College and her students, who took us on as their Spring Project, profiling our business and offering a storehouse of knowledge toward projections of market analysis.

We must thank the First Union Bank for their advisory expertise and support of that market analysis. With their assistance, we charted our course, kept our minds on the target, and worked toward our goal. Special thanks to Doug McCoy and Eric Waters.

The Small Business Administration Corporation supported our dreams and worked very closely with us. We appreciate their vision and look forward to attaining new goals in the future. Special thanks to Steven George and Tony O'Rielly.

The *Savannah News Press* has so generously provided exceptional reviews for our restaurant, and for that, we are grateful.

Thanks also to Karl Schumacher, CPA, for his continued advice and support over the years.

[1997]

The Lady & Sons Restaurant
102 West Congress Street
Savannah, GA 31401
912-233-2600 Fax 912-232-5522

Table of Contents

OFFICE OF THE MAYOR
CITY OF SAVANNAH

FLOYD ADAMS, JR., MAYOR

February 7, 1997

CONGRATULATIONS!

Dear Lady & Sons:

The City of Savannah is delighted to recognize you as one of the best new restaurants. We are proud that you have decided to invest in Savannah and to let Savannah enjoy your excellent selection of food.

The Lady & Sons offers a marvelous variety of delicious home-made dishes, but also a wide assortment of international dishes. City Council has been enjoying these magnificent treats during the past year and we look forward to many more.

All of us join in thanking you and wishing you the best of success for the coming years.

Sincerely,

Floyd Adams, Jr.
Mayor

FA:pb

Introduction

I remember my maternal grandparents and stories of The White House Restaurant in Albany, Georgia, where I grew up. Grandmother Paul was a wonderful cook, and she handed down this talent and love of cooking to her three daughters: my mother and my two aunts. They, in turn, passed this love to me. My life has been surrounded by good cooks from both my mother's and my father's families, and I have been greatly blessed by these wonderful cooks and close family members.

I wanted to try a different line of work, however, and took a job in a bank. I learned a lot about managing money, but I very quickly decided I was in the wrong place when I was held hostage with a gun at the side of my head while the bank was robbed.

In 1989, I saw my life changing drastically. Unemployed, with only $200 initial investment, but a firm determination to create a secure future for myself and my sons, Jamie and Bobby, I decided to follow in Grandmother Paul's footsteps and become a restaurant owner.

To obtain my license in the food-preparation industry, I utilized the kitchen facilities of a restaurant on State Street after-hours. After obtaining my license, I cooked each night until as late as 3 o'clock in the morning to fill orders for the following day. The prepared meals were packed in ice and ready for the microwave! With the help of my two sons and two "girl-friends-in-law," the lunches were delivered to beauty shops (for patrons who got their hair done on lunch breaks), attorney offices, and other businesses. Thus was born The Bag Lady, which soon grew into The Lady & Sons.

The Lady & Sons has served many political dignitaries, Hollywood actors and actresses, tour guests, and Olympic guests from around the world, as well as our own downtown patrons. We are fortunate to have a working staff dedicated to providing the finest home-cooked meals in an atmosphere of true Southern hospitality. The Lady & Sons was voted the best new restaurant for 1996 by the *Savannah Morning News* Opinion Poll.

I hope my story will inspire others to accept challenges and make good things happen in their own lives. The artistic humor depicted in this cookbook is intended to show that cooking can be more than a chore — it can be fun!

Paula H. Deen

[1997]

A Special Tribute...

We would like to share a special story with you about our mother, Paula Hiers Deen. She is truly a symbol of strength and perseverance. One must have extraordinary strength of character to ask for help and be refused. It takes strong courage to achieve goals when doors are slammed in your face and no one seems to believe in your dreams or capabilities; but our mother has done just that.

This book is a product of her twenty-hour workdays. This book is her "third child," and she has nourished and cherished it just as she has cared for her two sons, in a way that only a mother could do. This book stretches across many years and different situations: years of being a struggling homemaker, a bank teller, and a worker for a temporary service; days of hard work, dreaming and planning for the future.

But, thanks to our mother, these are now the best days of our lives. We have more pride in this lady than anyone else on earth. She has our undying adoration and our commitment to follow her direction. Anyone in America can accomplish anything they set out to do if they have the sincere desire to succeed. Mother is a remarkable lady. We hope you enjoy her first cookbook.

We love you, Mom

Jamie and Bobby
[1997]

A tribute to My Sons

It's been twenty years, but I remember it like it was yesterday, that exciting day Jamie, Bobby, and I walked down the block, holding hands, to pick up the first three copies of *Favorite Recipes of The Lady & Her Friends*, hot off the press. Jamie turned to me and said, "Momma, you are gonna cry when you get your book." I said, "No I'm not. I'm so happy to have this done." He said, "I'll bet you $100 you are gonna cry." I opened the book to page 6, where Jamie and Bobby had secretly asked the printer to add "A Special Tribute," and I lost $100.

So this time, Momma turns the tables on them. Jamie and Bobby will have no idea this page exists until they hold this book in their hands, just like I did twenty years ago.

It's hard for me to put into words the love I have for my sons and the pride in them I feel. To try to describe what it's like as a parent to have your children by your side and to be basically penniless is difficult—we had no financial security at all. And for them to step up to the side of their mother and roll up their sleeves and be willing to work hard to build a future for us and their families has just—it just makes my heart go into overload. You can't put into words how that makes you feel. My children and I are truly a team; and it's one for all, and all for one. I have been blessed—overblessed—with the way my sons have turned out. As Jackie Kennedy said years ago, "If you bungle raising your children, I don't think whatever else you do matters very much." The most important thing one can do in this world is raise good, responsible children. My Jamie and Bobby came from a dysfunctional home, but somehow they rose above it, and for that I am very, very thankful. They make me proud every day.

Paula H. Deen

2017

In 2012, I established The Bag Lady Foundation, named after my first business, to provide hope, inspiration, and support to women and families during their time of need. The Bag Lady Foundation receives funding through charitable contributions as well as a portion of proceeds from Paula Deen Foods.

Suggestions from the lady

1. Unless specifically instructed to put your dish in a cold oven to begin baking it, you should *always preheat* the oven to the temperature required.

2. Beat eggs; then add sugar.

3. Combine dry ingredients together.

4. Add flour and milk to egg mixture, alternately, beginning with flour mixture and ending with flour mixture.

5. To eliminate odor from collards being cooked, add one washed unshelled pecan to the collards pot.

6. To determine whether an egg is fresh or not, place the uncracked egg in a glass of water. If it sinks to the bottom, it's fresh. If it floats, throw it out!

7. To make fluffier scrambled eggs, beat in a small amount of water instead of milk.

8. If baking a double-crust pie, brush top layer lightly with milk for a shiny crust; for a sweet crust, sprinkle with granulated sugar or a mixture of sugar and cinnamon; for a glazed crust, brush lightly with beaten egg. Placing a cookie sheet in the oven during preheating will ensure that the bottom crust will bake through.

9. Substitute 1⅔ cups all-purpose flour for 2 cups cake flour.

10. No buttermilk? Add 1 teaspoon vinegar to 1 cup fresh milk; let sour.

11. 1½ cups corn syrup equals 1 cup sugar plus ½ cup water.

12. To remove excess grease from soups, drop in a lettuce leaf and watch it absorb the grease. Repeat until the desired amount is removed. Discard lettuce.

13. For unused egg yolks, place in bowl and cover with 2 tablespoons of oil. They will remain fresh for future use.

14. In the middle of making a pecan pie, only to find someone has eaten the pecans?? Don't fret, substitute crushed cornflakes for the pecans. Bake as usual.

15. 1 cup tomato juice equals ½ cup tomato sauce plus ½ cup water.

[1997]

Secrets from the Lady

Cheese Biscuits: Even though the recipe calls for self-rising flour, I add a little baking powder to make them rise more. This secret can be applied to any recipe calling for self-rising flour or self-rising meal if you want to achieve a lighter texture in your baking.

Always out of condensed milk? Make your own. Mix 6 cups whole milk with 4½ cups sugar, 1 stick of butter, and 1 vanilla bean (or equivalent substitute). Cook over medium heat, reducing liquid, for 1 hour. Stir occasionally. Cool. Yields 4½ cups. This can be stored covered in the refrigerator for several weeks. Cut recipe in half for immediate use.

Red potatoes are far superior for use in any potato recipe. For great convenience in preparing a variety of potato recipes, keep cooked red potatoes in the refrigerator at all times. They can be used on the spur of the moment for potato salad; hash browns; sliced, for French fries; and crushed and added to milk, salt, and pepper for a wonderful cream of potato soup. They will keep at least a week in the refrigerator if they are well drained.

Rub uncooked potatoes with melted butter, sprinkle with Kosher salt, and bake uncovered for the best baked potato ever. Can also be cooked in the microwave.

In most of the recipes by The Lady, you will find we make reference to our House Seasoning. The recipe is 1 cup salt, ¼ cup black pepper, and ¼ cup garlic powder.

Flavored Whipped Cream: Use different liqueurs to flavor a whipped topping for your desserts. We have used crème de cassis in whipped cream over blueberries; Calvados cream over apple pie or apple desserts; and grenadine over cherries. *The method:* Whip in 2 tablespoons liqueur to 1 cup whipping cream. Drizzle a little extra liqueur over the top for added taste and presentation. *A special we like:* To 1 cup whipping cream, add 2 tablespoons cocoa and ⅓ cup sugar for a chocolate topping. For Kahlúa whipped cream, use 1 cup whipping cream, 2 tablespoons sugar, and 2 tablespoons Kahlúa liqueur. For plain sweetened whipped cream, I always use 1 cup heavy whipping cream, ¼ cup sugar, and 1 teaspoon vanilla extract. Have fun with this; let us know what new uses you discover.

[1997]

Comments from our Guests

"Good variety of excellent food. All was very good, especially butter beans with ham hock and collard greens." ...Mr. and Mrs. White, DE

"The hoe cakes were the first I've had in more than 15 years. If memory serves me well, and I believe it does, they were as good as my dear mother's."
...Dianne Norman, Jacksonville, FL

"Thanks for a great lunch served by a special lady, Maria." ...Jesse and Georgina

"Doggone Good!" ...Michael and Doretha

"Great home cooking. Very enjoyable." ...Pat Watkins

"The hoe cakes are the most decadent non-dessert in the world. Ten of them and two pieces of fried chicken plus sweet tea w/mint, and 'Go Home, Mama!'"
...Jeff Forslund, Charleston, SC

"An essential part of Savannah's community!" ...Dan Simmons, Savannah, GA

"The food at Lady & Sons is just fantastic. I've eaten here for over six months, and everything is just perfect. Try the biscuits or fried green tomatoes!"
...Susie Drayton Harris, Savannah, GA

"Full, Full, Full; Diet, Diet, Diet!" ...Susan DiDi Marino

"First real Southern food with a lot of taste! Congrats on the award as #1!"

"Southwest Georgia has finally moved East! ...Great!" ...Bob Christian

"Food is great; very attractive." ...A.R.S.

"Every time I come into this place, I leave with a smile on my face."

"No one in this town does it better!" ...Stanton Jaye, Savannah, GA

"The hoe cakes were out of this world! The food, service, and atmosphere are outstanding. We will be back."

"When you eat at The Lady & Sons, it's like being home at the dinner table. Thanks for a good home-cooked meal." ...C. Sample

"It is like going to see my grandmother in Macon."
...Margaret Nelson, Savannah, GA

"I would like a larger plate, please!"   ...David Guggenhein, Savannah, GA

"Absolutely fabulous!! The lima beans were the best I've ever had. Even my husband, who hates lima beans, would like these! Thanks!"
...Melanie O'Brien, Atlanta, GA

"Delicious! I would walk miles just for a taste of those cheese biscuits!"
...Tommy Edenfield, Savannah, GA

"The Lady & Sons staff knows how to handle the crowd during lunchtime, and that is great! Keep up the good work."   ...Japonica Jenkins

"Excellent vegetables and overall nice atmosphere."
...Eric Pollak, Darroll Coffee

"Everything was delicious—good food, service, and atmosphere."
...Trudy Duffy, Hilton Head, SC

"Very friendly, great service. Crab cakes to die for. Just as good as the Chesapeake Bay crabs."   ...Chris Walish, Los Angeles and Maryland

"Biscuits are unbelievable! Best ever."   ...Janet Burns, Springfield, VA

"From one good cook to another: It was terrific! Can't wait to get your recipe book."   ...Dianna Sakacs, Lanham, MD

"Macaroni and cheese—it's great!"

"The food was great. The place is beautiful and comfortable, and the waiter/waitresses are as nice as can be. It was a pleasure. Thanks!"
...Stan and Aleve Weinstein, NYC, NY

"Ran out of the best ribs I've had in a long, long time. Biscuits—Wow!!!"
...Opal Wiita, Canton, OH

"Excellent cheese biscuits and limas....Suggest a plate just for biscuits, corn bread, and syrup."   ...Lauritta Fleming, Conway, MI

"The service and food are equally superb!"

"This is the sweetest cookin' east of the Mississippi. 'Good ol' Southern Hospitality' defines The Lady & Sons."   ...Alicia O. Richards

"I have eaten at The Lady twice for lunch. Both times, the food was excellent. It was seasoned to perfection, and it was very tasty." ...Mary Ann Coleman

"Food is excellent; waiters/waitresses are exceptional. Only second to my mother's home; the best of the rest in Savannah." ...Earnestine Baker

"I do not know how you make your creamed corn, but please come home with me." ...Michael Barker, Savannah, GA

"It was very good. Wonderful food!" ...Nita H. Miller

"It's great. Everything is excellent."

"There's only one other place that feeds me like this, but Mom doesn't cook for me anymore."

"Wonderful food and service. Mom doesn't cook dinner when we lunch here."
...John Walsh

"The crab cakes were the best we have ever had." ...Cynthia and Sal Vincent

"Southern cooking has NEVER been this good!" ...Ben Price

"Never eaten better!" ...Carl Blair, Clerk of State Court

"Dining at The Lady & Sons reminds me of Sunday dinner at my grandmother's. Take a trip into your past: have lunch or dinner at The Lady & Sons and remember those great Sunday meals at your grandmother's home." ...Bill Ball Jr.

"True Southern cooking and true Southern hospitality. Oh, so good!"
...Miles and Bonnie Harrison

"An institution in its own right ... and a befitting complement to the fine Southern tradition of Savannah." ...W. Hodges, MD, PhD

"So very much like the food I grew up on. The hoe cakes are excellent, and 'thank you' for the Southern-style vegetables." ...Gerald Benson, DDS

[1997]

Appetizers & Beverages

A toast....

Among the things that good wine brings,. What better than laughter, That rings in revery, That makes better friends of you & me?

PECAN-STUFFED DATES

1 8-ounce box pitted dates	10 to 12 slices bacon
30 pecan halves	

Preheat oven to 400 degrees. Stuff each date with a pecan half. Cut each slice of bacon into 3 pieces. Wrap 1 piece around each stuffed date and secure with a toothpick. Bake until bacon is crisp, 12 to 15 minutes. Drain and serve.

the Lady

CHICKEN NUGGETS

2 cups crushed sour-cream-and- onion-flavored potato chips	6 chicken breast fillets, cut into 1½-inch cubes
1 egg	⅓ cup butter, melted
2 tablespoons milk	

Preheat oven to 350 degrees. Spread crushed potato chips in a shallow dish. In a shallow bowl, beat together egg and milk. Dip chicken cubes into egg mixture and dredge in chips. Place chicken nuggets on a baking sheet and drizzle with melted butter. Bake for 15 to 18 minutes, or until golden brown. Chicken nuggets can be frozen after baking. Serve with your favorite sauce, such as honey mustard or ranch dressing.

Marion Streiner, Hilton Head, SC

TERIYAKI SPARERIB APPETIZERS

3 pounds pork spare ribs	½ cup prepared teriyaki sauce
Salt and pepper to taste	¼ cup orange marmalade

Lightly sprinkle spareribs with salt and pepper; cut into 1 or 2 rib portions. Place on rack in foil-lined broiler pan. Bake at 325 degrees for 45 minutes. Mix teriyaki sauce and orange marmalade; brush both sides of ribs with mixture. Bake 1 hour more, turning over frequently to brush with sauce mixture.

Kelley Ort, Atlanta, GA

Kelley is married to my cousin George, and she is an amazing cook.

HOT HAM AND CHEESE SANDWICHES

1 stick butter, at room temperature	1 tablespoon poppy seeds
¼ cup prepared mustard	8 hamburger buns
¼ cup chopped onion	8 slices Swiss cheese
	8 slices boiled ham

Mix first four ingredients together and spread inside hamburger buns. Place a slice of Swiss cheese and boiled ham in each. Wrap individual sandwiches in aluminum foil and bake at 350 degrees for 20 minutes.

Elizabeth Denny Adams (Mrs. John L.), Savannah, GA

ONION QUICHE (PARTY SIZE)

¾ cup crushed saltine crackers	2 eggs
½ stick butter, melted	1 cup milk
1 cup chopped green onion with tops	½ teaspoon salt
2 tablespoons butter	¼ teaspoon pepper
	1 cup grated Swiss cheese

Preheat oven to 300 degrees. Combine cracker crumbs and melted butter. Divide crumbs among mini muffin tins that have been sprayed with no-stick cooking spray. Sauté onion for 10 minutes in 2 tablespoons butter. Cool, then divide evenly on top of cracker crumbs. Beat eggs; add milk, salt, pepper, and Swiss cheese. Pour by spoonfuls on top of onion in tins. Do not fill to top, as they will run over. Bake until set, about 15 to 20 minutes. Do not overbake. May be stored in refrigerator or freezer. Warm in oven before serving.

the lady

DIANNE'S SUGARED PEANUTS

Dianne and I grew up together and she is a dear friend. She now resides in Atlanta, but we have been friends since childhood.

1 cup sugar	2 cups raw shelled peanuts, skins on
½ cup water	¼ teaspoon salt

Preheat oven to 300 degrees. Dissolve sugar and salt in water in saucepan over medium heat. Add peanuts. Continue to cook, stirring frequently, until peanuts are completely sugared (coated and no syrup left). Pour onto ungreased cookie sheet, spreading so that peanuts are separated as much as possible. Bake for approximately 30 minutes, stirring at 5-minute intervals. Let cool and serve.

Dianne Tedder, Atlanta, GA

MOCK GUACAMOLE SPINACH DIP

1 package dry guacamole dip mix (found in produce departments)
1 8-ounce container soft cream cheese
1 10-ounce package frozen chopped spinach, thawed
1 large tomato, finely chopped

Combine guacamole mix and cream cheese. Squeeze excess liquid from spinach. Add to cheese mixture. Add tomato. Mix well to combine. Serve with tortilla chips.

Kelley Ort, Atlanta, GA

ARTICHOKE/SPINACH DIP

Sheila is the daughter of a longtime friend. She is fast becoming a favorite caterer in Albany, Georgia.

½ 10-ounce package frozen chopped spinach, thawed	½ cup mayonnaise
	½ cup sour cream
2 13¾-ounce cans artichoke hearts, drained and mashed	1½ cups grated Parmesan cheese
	Salt and pepper to taste

Preheat oven to 350 degrees. Drain all water from spinach. Mix all ingredients and bake in greased casserole for 30 to 40 minutes. Serve with butter crackers or bagel chips.

Sheila Mims, Albany, GA

SAUSAGE BALLS
An old standard; easy recipe.

3 cups Bisquick	1 pound fresh ground sausage
2 cups grated Cheddar cheese	(hot or mild)

Preheat oven to 350 degrees. Mix all ingredients together. If not moist enough, add a little water. Form mixture into 1-inch balls. Bake for 15 minutes. Drain on paper towels. Serve warm. This freezes well before or after baking. *the lady*

MONTEZ'S HAM-CHEESE LOGS

1 cup shredded sharp Cheddar cheese, at room temperature	1 4½-ounce can deviled ham
1 8-ounce package cream cheese, at room temperature	½ cup chopped pitted green olives
	½ cup finely chopped pecans

In a small bowl, blend together Cheddar and cream cheeses. Beat in deviled ham, then stir in olives. Refrigerate mixture for at least 2 hours, or until firm enough to slice. Shape cheese mixture into two 8-inch logs. Roll cheese logs in chopped nuts. Serve with crackers. *the lady*

SWEDISH MEATBALLS

3 slices bread, crumbled	2 tablespoons vegetable oil, plus small amount for browning meatballs
⅓ cup milk	
1 pound ground beef	
1 small onion, grated	1 8-ounce package gravy mix
½ teaspoon salt	½ cup mayonnaise
¼ teaspoon pepper	Dash of ground nutmeg

Add bread to milk. Mix together ground beef, onion, salt, pepper, and 2 tablespoons of the vegetable oil; shape into 1-inch balls and chill. In a large skillet, brown meatballs in oil. Prepare gravy as directed on package, using 1¼ cups water. Blend in mayonnaise and nutmeg. Add to meatballs and heat. Serve hot in chafing dish. *the lady*

ADRIENNE'S DELIGHT

12 ounces cream cheese
1   stick butter
½   cup sour cream
½   cup sugar
1   envelope plain gelatin

¼   cup cold water
¼   cup white raisins
1   cup slivered toasted
    almonds (optional)
Zest from 2 lemons

Let cream cheese, butter, and sour cream come to room temperature; cream well; add sugar and combine. Soften gelatin in cold water; place over hot water to dissolve. Add to cream cheese mixture. Mixture will be runny. Add raisins, almonds (if desired), and lemon zest. Place in a 1-quart mold and refrigerate until firm. Unmold on serving tray. Serve with crackers. May be frozen.

SPICED TEA

1   18-ounce jar Tang
1   cup instant lemon-flavored tea
2   teaspoons ground cinnamon

1   teaspoon ground cloves
½   teaspoon ground nutmeg

Combine all ingredients and store in air-tight container. To serve, place 1 or 2 tablespoonfuls in coffee mug. Add hot water for a delightful, spicy drink.

the Lady

PICKLED-OKRA SANDWICHES

1   24-ounce loaf sliced white bread
1   8-ounce package cream cheese,
    softened

1   16-ounce jar pickled okra
1   cup finely chopped fresh
    parsley

Remove crusts from bread. With a rolling pin, roll slices very thin. Coat each slice with cream cheese and place an okra spear in center; roll up. Spread a light coat of cream cheese on each rolled-up sandwich (I like to use my fingers to spread the cream cheese). Roll sandwich in finely chopped parsley. Cut in half, if desired.

the Lady

STUFFED MUSHROOMS

24 fresh mushrooms, stems
   removed
1 10-ounce package frozen
   chopped spinach
2 ounces cream cheese

4 ounces feta cheese
½ cup finely chopped green
   onion with tops
   Salt to taste
1 cup grated Parmesan cheese

Preheat oven to 350 degrees. Wipe mushroom caps clean with a damp
paper towel. Thaw spinach in colander; squeeze out as much moisture as
possible. In mixing bowl, combine all ingredients except mushrooms and
Parmesan cheese. Mix well. Fill mushroom caps with mixture and place
on a cookie sheet. Sprinkle Parmesan cheese on top. Bake for 15 to
20 minutes. Serve warm.   *the Lady*

CRAB DIP

1 pound crab meat (claw meat)
1 cup Hellmann's mayonnaise
1 tablespoon horseradish sauce
1½ cups grated Cheddar cheese

Dash of Tabasco
Dash of lemon juice
Dash of Worcestershire
sauce

Blend all ingredients together. Use Worcestershire sauce, Tabasco, and
lemon juice to taste. Serve cold.   *Rose Mary Lee, Savannah, GA*

HOT ASPARAGUS HORS D'OEVOURS
*This is exactly identical to our artichoke dip. It is a nice,
refreshing change.*

2 12-ounce cans asparagus spears
1½ cups mayonnaise
1½ cups freshly grated Parmesan
   cheese

2 cloves garlic, chopped
   Salt and pepper to taste

Preheat oven to 350 degrees. Drain and chop asparagus. Add to remaining
ingredients and mix; pour into baking dish. Bake for 20 to 25 minutes until
slightly brown and bubbly. Remove from oven and sprinkle with additional
Parmesan cheese. Serve hot with lightly toasted French bread rounds.
                                                            the Lady

BACON ROLL-UPS

12 slices white bread
1 can cream of mushroom soup

12 thin slices bacon

Trim crust off bread; cut each slice diagonally into 2 triangles. Spread each piece with 1 teaspoon soup. Fold three corners together, wrap with ½ slice bacon, and secure with a toothpick. Cook in slow 250-degree oven for 2½ hours. Makes 48 roll-ups. Prepare these the night before, and serve to children while they are opening gifts on Christmas morning. A family favorite!

the lady

FESTIVE FRUIT PUNCH

1 46-ounce can orange juice
1 46-ounce can pineapple juice
1 pint lemon juice
1 quart sugar
1 tablespoon vanilla extract

1 tablespoon almond flavoring
1 quart ginger ale
1 46-ounce can water
1 Ice Mold

In large punch bowl, combine all ingredients above; mix well. Add Ice Mold and serve.

Ice Mold: Combine 7-Up, orange slices, maraschino cherries, lemon slices, mint leaves, and strawberries in a festive mold. Freeze until ready to use.

the lady

RUBY WINE PUNCH

1 4- to 5-quart bottle claret or Burgundy, chilled
3 cups orange juice, chilled

⅓ cup lemon juice
½ cup sugar
1 1-quart bottle ginger ale, chilled

In a punch bowl, combine wine, orange juice, lemon juice, and sugar; stir until sugar is dissolved. Add a block of ice or ice cubes. Pour in ginger ale just before serving. Makes about 25 to 30 3-ounce servings.

the lady

PEACH MELBA WITH PORT

For each serving, lay one or two chilled, cooked, or canned peach halves, cut side up, in dessert dish. Top with a scoop of vanilla ice cream and cover with Port Sauce.

Port Sauce

1	#2 can red raspberries	1	tablespoon butter
4	tablespoons cornstarch	2	tablespoons lemon juice
¼	cup sugar	¼	cup port wine
	Dash of salt		

Force raspberries through a sieve fine enough to remove all seeds. Mix cornstarch, sugar, and salt in a saucepan; stir in raspberry puree; and cook, stirring constantly, until mixture boils. Remove from heat; add butter and stir until melted. Add lemon juice and port wine. Chill before serving. Makes about 2 cups sauce. Excellent with other fruit desserts and puddings.

the lady

MARY'S BANANA BERRY SHAKE

½	small container frozen strawberries	1	banana, mashed
		½	cup apple juice

Combine ingredients in blender. Add a small handful of ice. Blend well.

Mary Bridger, Albany, GA

BOURBON WEINER SURPRISE

2	packages 50-count Lil' Link weiners	2	jars chili sauce
1	pint bourbon	2	cups brown sugar

Place weiners in baking dish. Mix bourbon, chili sauce, and brown sugar. Pour over weiners, making sure all are coated well. Bake at 300 degrees for 2 hours, until sauce is thickened.

Aileen Patton, Carson, CA

✓ Twenty years ago, there were Lil' Link weiners. Today, use any mini hot dogs.

EASY BAKED CHEESE SPREAD

Nancy and I met during the "Bag Lady" days. Our original contact was business oriented, but now she is a good friend and a good cook and she knows good food.

1   cup mayonnaise
1   cup grated Colby cheese
1   cup chopped onion

Dash of Tabasco (optional)
Dash of Worcestershire
sauce (optional)

Preheat oven to 350 degrees. Mix all ingredients in a pie plate. Bake until golden brown on top, about 30 minutes. Serve with crackers or bagel chips.   *Nancy Blood, Savannah, GA*

STUFFED FRENCH BREAD

3   small loaves French bread, each approximately 6 inches long
2   8-ounce packages cream cheese, at room temperature
1   cup mayonnaise

1   2-ounce jar pimentos, drained and chopped
⅓   cup chopped fresh parsley
1   0.7-ounce package Italian salad dressing mix
1   2¼-ounce jar of chopped dried beef (optional)

Cut each loaf in half lengthwise. Remove some of the inside bread to make room for stuffing. Combine remaining ingredients and mix well. Fill hollows in bread with mixture. Reassemble bread into loaves. Wrap in plastic wrap and refrigerate until ready to serve, at least 3 hours. To serve, slice loaves into 1-inch sections.   *Kelley Ort, Atlanta, GA*

LAYERED MEXICAN DIP

3   ripe avocados, peeled and mashed
2   tablespoons fresh lemon juice
    Pinch of garlic salt
    Pinch of black pepper
    Dash of hot sauce
1   cup sour cream
1   cup mayonnaise
1   1¼-ounce package taco seasoning
4   9-ounce cans Frito-Lay bean dip
1   16-ounce jar picante sauce,
    or salsa, drained
1   cup chopped yellow onion
    or green onion
3   tomatoes, chopped
1   6-ounce can pitted black
    olives, drained
    Sliced jalapeño peppers
    to taste (optional)
8   ounces sharp Cheddar
    cheese, grated
4   ounces Monterey Jack
    cheese, grated

In a bowl, stir together avocado, lemon juice, garlic salt, black pepper, and hot sauce; set aside. In another bowl, mix sour cream, mayonnaise, and taco seasoning; set aside. In a wide, shallow bowl, layer bean dip, avocado mixture, sour-cream mixture, picante sauce, onion, tomatoes, olives, and jalapeño peppers (if desired), and top with both cheeses. Serve with tortilla chips.   *Nancy Blood, Savannah, GA*

JEANNENE'S CHRISTMAS CHEESE

1   8-ounce package cream cheese,
    softened
1   pound American cheese, grated
½ to ¾ large can evaporated milk
2   cloves garlic, minced
½   teaspoon salt
1   cup chopped ripe olives
1   cup chopped pecans
    Paprika

Beat together cream cheese, American cheese, milk, garlic, and salt. Add olives and pecans; mix with your hands. Form into loaves and sprinkle heavily with paprika. Wrap in waxed paper; chill.
                                    Kelley Ort, Atlanta, GA

SPICED PECANS

1	cup sugar	2	cups pecan halves
½	teaspoon ground cinnamon	1	teaspoon vanilla extract
⅓	cup evaporated milk		

In a medium saucepan, combine sugar, cinnamon, and milk. Bring to a boil and cook to soft-ball stage (234 to 238 degrees on a candy thermometer). Add pecans and vanilla and stir well. Using a slotted spoon, drop single pecans on a sheet of waxed paper; allow to cool.   *Kelley Ort, Atlanta, GA*

OYSTERS IN THE PATTY SHELL

½	pound mushrooms, chopped	1	cup shelled fresh oysters, drained and chopped
3	tablespoons butter		
3	tablespoons all-purpose flour	8	1-ounce prebaked mini-piecrusts or patty shells (approximately 3-inch diameter)
1	cup milk		
½	teaspoon salt		
¼	teaspoon celery salt		
	Pepper to taste		Fresh parsley, for garnish
1	teaspoon lemon juice		

Sauté mushrooms in butter until tender. Blend in flour and cook until bubbly. Gradually add milk; cook until smooth and thickened, stirring constantly. Add salt, celery salt, pepper, lemon juice, and oysters. Cook over medium-low heat until oysters start to curl up (about 5 minutes), stirring occasionally. Serve in mini-piecrusts or patty shells. If desired, garnish with parsley.   *Kelley Ort, Atlanta, GA*

PESTO AND CREAM CHEESE ROUND

2	8-ounce packages cream cheese, softened	1	tablespoon dried basil
1	cup chopped fresh parsley	¼	teaspoon salt
¾	cup grated Parmesan cheese	⅛	teaspoon pepper
¼	cup chopped pine nuts	⅓	cup olive oil
2	cloves garlic, crushed	2	tablespoons butter, melted
		2	tablespoons boiling water

Shape cream cheese into a 5½-inch circle on serving dish, making a slight well in center of circle; set aside. Combine parsley with rest of ingredients. Mix well. Spoon onto cream cheese round; garnish with fresh basil sprigs if desired. Cover and chill at least 2 hours. Serve with crackers or toasted pita triangles.

Kelley Ort, Atlanta, GA

PUNCH FOR 150 PEOPLE

6	pounds sugar	1	large can orange juice
4	ounces citric acid	2	large cans pineapple juice

Add 4 quarts boiling water to sugar and citric acid. Let stand overnight. Next day, add 8 quarts cold water and juices. This punch can be served with champagne, vodka, etc. DO NOT mix in aluminum: use enamel or crockery.

Peggy Ort, Albany, GA

HOLIDAY PUNCH

2	cups cranberries	2	tablespoons lemon juice or orange juice
3	cups water		
½	cup sugar	1	pint lime sherbet

Cook cranberries in water until very soft; strain, saving juice. Combine juice and sugar. Cook until sugar is dissolved, about 5 minutes. Chill. Add lemon or orange juice to taste. Pour into punch bowl. Float scoops of lime sherbet on top. To serve, ladle juice and sherbet into cups. Serves 8. Serve this punch at the holidays, when cranberries are fresh and plentiful.

Diane Silver Berryhill, Savannah, GA

CORRIE'S EGGNOG

This recipe brings back many wonderful memories from my childhood. It represents very festive occasions, and I remember Mama serving this cool, frothy eggnog to her guests. The laughter and happy times are very strong memories today.

6	eggs, separated	½	pint bourbon
¾	cup sugar	1	teaspoon vanilla extract
1	pint heavy cream		Ground nutmeg to taste
1	pint milk		(optional)

In a bowl, beat egg yolks with ½ cup of the sugar until thick. In another bowl, beat egg whites with ¼ cup of the sugar until thick. In a third bowl, beat cream until thick. Add cream to yolks; fold in egg whites. Add milk, bourbon, and vanilla. Add nutmeg, if desired. Chill in freezer.

Aunt Trina Bearden, Houma, LA
(Mother's younger sister)

Trina was only three years older than me, and although she was my aunt, we grew up as sisters. We honor her memory by cherishing her many wonderful recipes.

Salads & Salad Dressing

"the quickest way to a man's ~~wallet~~ heart is through his stomach——"

CORRIE'S JELL-O SALAD

1	3-ounce package lemon Jell-O	1	cup mayonnaise
1	3-ounce package lime Jell-O	½	cup orange juice
1	20-ounce can crushed pineapple	½	cup pecan pieces
1	16-ounce carton cottage cheese	1	teaspoon horseradish

Dissolve lemon and lime Jell-O in 2 cups hot water; pour into 13×9-inch casserole. Refrigerate until slightly jelled. Add remaining ingredients and stir gently. Return to refrigerator until completely set.

SAUERKRAUT SALAD

2	pounds loose kraut, well drained	1	bell pepper, chopped
1	small onion, finely chopped	1	cup chopped celery
			Salad dressing

In large serving bowl, combine kraut, onion, bell pepper, and celery; toss well. Add salad dressing. Mix well, serve.

Dressing

1¼	cups sugar	⅔	cup water
⅓	cup vinegar	½	cup salad oil

Alberta DiClaudio, Savannah, GA

PASTA SALAD

1	16-ounce box angel hair pasta, cooked according to instructions	¾	cup vegetable oil
1	4-ounce jar sliced pimentos	3	tablespoons mayonnaise
8	green onions, chopped	4	tablespoons fresh lemon juice
1	3-ounce jar sliced black olives, drained	4	tablespoons broiled steak seasoning salt
			Black pepper to taste
			Dash of Tabasco

Combine first four ingredients and set aside. Mix together vegetable oil, mayonnaise, lemon juice, steak seasoning salt, black pepper, and Tabasco; whisk until well blended. Pour over pasta mixture.

Amy Beaver, Albany, GA

MARINATED CARROTS (COPPER PENNIES)

1   cup sugar
¾   cup white vinegar
½   cup vegetable oil
1   teaspoon dry mustard
1   teaspoon Worcestershire sauce
1   teaspoon salt
¾   teaspoon coarsely ground
    black pepper

1   10¾-ounce can tomato soup
2   pounds carrots, peeled,
    cooked, and sliced
1   medium onion, sliced
    into rings
1   green bell pepper,
    coarsely chopped

In a saucepan over medium heat, combine sugar, vinegar, oil, mustard, Worcestershire sauce, salt, and black pepper, and bring to a boil. Remove from heat and add soup. In a large glass dish, mix carrots, onion, and bell pepper. Pour sauce over vegetables, stir gently to combine, and refrigerate overnight. This salad will keep for up to 6 weeks in the refrigerator.

Sheila Mims, Albany, GA

STRAWBERRY CONGEALED SALAD

1   12-ounce container Cool Whip
1   14-ounce can sweetened
    condensed milk
1   8-ounce carton sour cream

1   21-ounce can strawberry
    pie filling
1   8½-ounce can crushed pineapple
1   cup chopped nuts

Mix all ingredients together and stir well. Pour into salad mold or individual salad molds. Refrigerate for at least 1 hour before serving.

Aunt Glennis Hiers, Statesboro, GA

JELL-O SALAD

3   boxes orange Jell-O mix
1   #2 can crushed pineapple
3   cups cold water

1   9-ounce container Cool Whip
1   cup grated Cheddar cheese
1   cup chopped nuts

In a saucepan over medium heat, mix Jell-O and pineapple until Jell-O is dissolved. Boil for 3 minutes; remove from heat. Add cold water; stir well. Add Cool Whip, Cheddar cheese, and nuts. Pour into mold and refrigerate until set.

Alberta DiClaudio, Savannah, GA

POTATO SALAD

8	medium red potatoes	1	teaspoon lemon-pepper
¼	cup chopped fresh parsley		seasoning
¼	cup chopped green onion tops	2	tablespoons Jane's Krazy
1	cup chopped celery		Mixed-Up Salt
3	hard-boiled eggs, chopped	1	tablespoon Dijon mustard
¼	cup chopped bell pepper	¼	cup mayonnaise
¼	cup diced pimentos	1	cup sour cream

Boil potatoes with skins on for 10 to 15 minutes, until tender. Let cool just to the touch and cut into cubes. In a large bowl, combine remaining ingredients. Add potatoes. Mix gently and serve at room temperature.

the lady

MIXED-FRUIT SALAD

1	1-pound bag frozen whole strawberries	1	20-ounce can chunky pineapple, drained
1	21-ounce can peach pie mix	1	pound seedless grapes
2	15¼-ounce cans lite chunky mixed fruit, drained		2 or 3 bananas, sliced

Combine first five ingredients in bowl. Refrigerate 2 hours. Before serving, add sliced bananas, toss, and serve.

the lady

FRUIT BOWL

3	tablespoons orange Tang Breakfast Drink mix	1	16-ounce can chunky mixed fruit, drained
1	15½-ounce can pineapple chunks, drained, juice reserved	1	11-ounce can mandarin oranges, drained
1	3.4-ounce box instant lemon pudding mix	1	6-ounce jar maraschino cherries
		3	large bananas

In a small bowl, stir Tang into reserved pineapple juice. Add lemon pudding mix and stir well. In a large bowl, combine pineapple, mixed fruit, oranges, and cherries, then mix fruit and pudding mixtures together; toss well. Refrigerate until ready to serve. Just before serving, slice and add bananas.

Mary Bridger, Albany, GA

ORANGE-WALNUT SALAD

Kelley is a super smart financial advisor and bank executive.
She is married to my cousin George Ort III. The mother of two
sons, she still makes time to produce wonderful gourmet dishes
for her family. Kelley has contributed several recipes to our book,
and I know you will enjoy trying all of them.

3 small heads Bibb lettuce, cleaned and torn into bite-size pieces	¾ medium red onion, sliced and separated into rings
1½ pounds fresh spinach, cleaned and torn into bite-size pieces	¾ cup coarsely chopped walnuts
3 oranges, peeled, sectioned, and seeded	3 teaspoons butter

Combine lettuce, spinach, oranges, and onion in a large bowl. In a
saucepan, sauté walnuts in butter until lightly browned. Add to lettuce
mixture. Toss with Sweet-and-Sour Dressing.   *Kelley Ort, Atlanta, GA*

COCA-COLA SALAD

6 ounces Coca-Cola	1 tablespoon chopped maraschino cherries
1 package lemon gelatin dissolved in 1 cup hot water	¼ cup chopped pecans
¼ cup chopped celery	Endive leaves, for serving
½ cup crushed pineapple, drained	

Add cola to gelatin and water. Refrigerate until thickened. Add remaining
ingredients, stirring in slowly. Pour into molds that have been chilled in
cold water. Chill until firm. Serve on endive. Serves 6.

Marella Walker, Emory University, Atlanta, GA

FRESH CRANBERRY SALAD

Crush 1 pound fresh cranberries in food grinder; spread 1 cup sugar over them. Leave in refrigerator overnight or for at least 2 hours. Then add 1 can crushed pineapple and 1 pound miniature marshmallows. Let sit for at least 2 more hours. Just before serving, fold in 1 cup coarsely chopped pecans and 1 pint stiffly whipped cream.

the lady

BROCCOLI SALAD

1 head broccoli	1 cup mayonnaise
6 to 8 slices cooked bacon, crumbled	2 tablespoons vinegar
½ cup chopped red onion	¼ cup sugar
½ cup raisins (optional)	1 cup halved cherry
8 ounces sharp Cheddar cheese, cut into very small chunks	tomatoes

Trim off large leaves of broccoli. Remove tough stalks at end and wash broccoli thoroughly. Cut flowerets and stems into bite-size pieces. Place in a large bowl. Add crumbled bacon, onion, raisins, and cheese. In a small bowl, combine remaining ingredients, stirring well. Add to broccoli mixture and toss gently.   *Terri Anderson Lister, Atlanta, GA*

ICE CREAM–PINEAPPLE MOLD

1 3-ounce package lime gelatin	1 cup crushed pineapple,
¾ cup boiling water	drained (optional)
1 pint vanilla ice cream	½ cup chopped nuts (optional)

Dissolve gelatin in boiling water. Add ice cream; stir until melted. Add pineapple and nuts, if desired. Stir until well mixed. Pour into mold that has been greased with a little salad dressing. Chill for 24 hours. Serves 6.
Violet Summerall, Hinesville, GA

CRANBERRY SALAD #1

1   4-ounce can crushed pineapple
1   3-ounce package black cherry
    Jell-O

6   ounces raw cranberries, rinsed
1   cup broken pecans
½   cup sugar

Drain pineapple and reserve juice. Add juice to ½ cup hot water and heat to boiling. Soften Jell-O in ¼ cup cold water. Dissolve softened Jell-O in hot water–juice mixture. Let cool until it starts to set; *don't let the Jell-O harden*. Put cranberries through a grinder. Add ground berries, pineapple, nuts, and sugar to cooled Jell-O mixture. Mix well. Pour into a bowl or mold. Refrigerate until completely set.   *Kelley Ort, Atlanta, GA*

CRANBERRY SALAD #2

1   6-ounce package cherry Jell-O
1   cup boiling water
1   cup cold water
1   14-ounce can whole cranberry
    sauce

1   20-ounce can crushed
    pineapple, *do not drain*
2   cups finely chopped celery
2   cups chopped nuts
    Juice and zest of 1 lemon

Mix all ingredients well. Pour into salad mold or 13×9-inch Pyrex dish. Refrigerate 2 to 3 hours.   *Martha Faulkner, Savannah, GA*

CONGEALED PISTACHIO SALAD

1   3.4-ounce box pistachio
    pudding mix
1   9-ounce package Cool Whip
1   cup marshmallows

1   15¼-ounce can crushed
    pineapple
1   cup chopped nuts

Mix all ingredients together and stir well. Pour into individual molds or one large mold. Refrigerate.   *the lady*

MAMA'S CONGEALED FRUIT SALAD

1½ cups boiling water
1   3-ounce package lemon gelatin
     dessert mix
1   3-ounce package lime gelatin
     dessert mix
1   20-ounce can crushed
     pineapple, drained
½   cup orange juice

½   cup evaporated milk
1   tablespoon fresh lemon juice
1   cup mayonnaise
½   cup cottage cheese
½   cup chopped walnuts
½   cup cherries, pitted, cut in half
     Prepared horseradish to taste
     Pinch of salt

In a large bowl, stir boiling water and gelatin mixes until dissolved. Let
cool slightly, then add pineapple, orange juice, evaporated milk, and
lemon juice. Refrigerate until slightly thickened. In a medium bowl, mix
together mayonnaise, cottage cheese, nuts, cherries, horseradish, and salt.
Stir mixture into gelatin. Pour into a lightly greased 13×9×2-inch pan and
refrigerate until firm.

COLESLAW
To me, the secret to good slaw is the way you cut your cabbage.
I have found that I prefer half of the cabbage coarsely chopped in a
food processor and half hand-sliced very thin. Use outside dark green
leaves, too, for color.

½   bell pepper, chopped
1   green onion, chopped
½   large carrot, chopped
⅛   cup chopped fresh parsley
½   head cabbage
½   cup mayonnaise

½   teaspoon Jane's Krazy Mixed-Up Salt
¼   teaspoon coarsely ground black
     pepper
2   tablespoons sugar
¼   teaspoon lemon-pepper seasoning
1 tablespoon white vinegar

In food processor, gently process bell pepper, onion, carrot, and parsley,
being careful not to overprocess (don't let mixture become mushy). Cut up
half the cabbage into chunks and place in food processor. Process lightly
(once again, don't let cabbage become mushy). Thinly slice remaining
cabbage. Mix the cabbage together, adding the processed vegetables.
Mix remaining ingredients together and allow to stand for a few minutes.
Pour over slaw ingredients and toss. Chill for at least an hour.

PRETZEL SALAD

2	cups crushed pretzels	2	3-ounce packages strawberry gelatin dessert mix
¾	cup butter, melted	2	cups boiling water
3	tablespoons plus ¾ cup sugar	2	10-ounce packages frozen strawberries
1	8-ounce package cream cheese	1	small can crushed pineapple
1	8-ounce carton Cool Whip		

Preheat oven to 400 degrees. For the crust, mix pretzels, butter, and 3 tablespoons sugar. Press mixture into bottom of a 13×9-inch pan. Bake for 7 minutes and set aside to cool. Beat together cream cheese and ¾ cup sugar. Fold in Cool Whip and spread over cooled crust. Refrigerate until well chilled. In a large bowl, dissolve gelatin dessert mix in boiling water; cool slightly. Add strawberries and pineapple, and pour over cream-cheese mixture. Refrigerate until serving time.   *Mary Bridger, Albany, GA*

AUNT PEGGY'S MARINATED GARDEN SALAD

1	2-ounce jar chopped pimentos	1	green bell pepper, chopped
1	14½-ounce can French green beans or Blue Lake beans, drained	¾	cup vinegar
1	15-ounce can Le Sueur English peas, drained	2	tablespoons cooking oil
1	cup chopped onion	1	cup sugar
1	cup chopped celery	1	teaspoon salt
		1	teaspoon black pepper

Combine first six ingredients in a large bowl. Bring to a boil the vinegar, oil, sugar, salt, and pepper; let cool. Pour over vegetables, stirring well. Place in a covered dish and let sit overnight in refrigerator.

Aunt Peggy Ort, Albany, GA

STRAWBERRY MOLD

2	3-ounce packages strawberry Jell-O	1	cup chopped pecans
1	cup boiling water	3	medium bananas, sliced
2	10-ounce cartons frozen strawberries	1	cup crushed pineapple, drained
		1	cup sour cream

Dissolve Jell-O in boiling water. Add remaining ingredients except sour cream. Pour half of mixture in salad mold; let chill. Cover with layer of sour cream, then top with remaining half of mixture. Refrigerate; chill until firm.

the lady

SODA CRACKER SALAD

This is a most unusual salad and quite delicious.
Thank you, Mary Evelyn, for sharing this family recipe.

1	sleeve saltine crackers	1½	cups mayonnaise
1	large tomato, finely chopped	1	hard-boiled egg, finely chopped
3	green onions, finely chopped		

Crush crackers. Mix all ingredients together and serve immediately.

Mary Evelyn Young, Sparks, GA

POTATO SALAD #1

6	cups diced new potatoes	4	hard-boiled eggs, chopped
⅓	cup Italian salad dressing	1	cup mayonnaise
1	teaspoon salt	½	cup sour cream
1	cup diced celery	1	teaspoon dry mustard
⅓	cup sliced green onions with tops	½	teaspoon horseradish

Boil potatoes with skins on for 15 to 20 minutes or until tender. Pour salad dressing over warm potatoes. Chill for about 2 hours. Mix remaining ingredients and fold into potato mixture. *Nancy Blood, Savannah, GA*

POTATO SALAD #2

8	large potatoes, boiled, cubed	2	teaspoons sugar
4	hard-boiled eggs, chopped	1	teaspoon salt
2	cups mayonnaise, or 1 cup mayo and 1 cup sour cream	¼	teaspoon pepper
		1	teaspoon fresh parsley
2	tablespoons cider vinegar (use less for blander taste)	2	teaspoons mustard
		½	cup chopped celery
1	envelope Hidden Valley dressing mix	½	cup chopped green pepper
		½	cup chopped green onion

Combine potatoes and eggs; toss lightly. Mix remaining ingredients and pour over potato mixture; toss lightly again.

Nancy Blood, Savannah, GA

THANKSGIVING APPLE SALAD

Sarah Phillips and Mary Williams are sisters and high school classmates of mine from years gone by. They went on to write a wonderful cookbook called Secret Ingredients. *This recipe was given to them, and we appreciate the opportunity to pass it on in our book. It is an excellent addition to any table, and the cherries lend such pretty color.*

¾	cup sugar	¼	cup butter
⅓	cup all-purpose flour	3 to 4	large red apples, diced
1	cup heavy cream	1	cup chopped nuts
1	20-ounce can crushed pineapple, drained	½	cup halved maraschino cherries

Stir together sugar and flour. Whisk in cream. Pour cream mixture into a heavy nonaluminum saucepan. Continue mixing, add pineapple, and cook over medium heat, whisking constantly, until mixture thickens. Add butter; remove pan from heat, and let mixture cool. When cooled, add apples, nuts, and cherries, and mix well. Refrigerate until ready to serve.

Mary Hulsey, Albany, GA

CONGEALED ASPARAGUS SALAD
Mr. and Mrs. Robertson are my brother Bubba's in-laws.
"Mr. and Miz Rob" have always been very dear to me.

2	envelopes plain gelatin	8	olives, sliced
¾	cup sugar	½	cup chopped pecans
1	cup water	1	2-ounce jar pimentos, chopped
½	cup white vinegar	1	15-ounce can green asparagus,
½	teaspoon salt		drained
1	cup chopped celery	2	teaspoons grated onion

Dissolve gelatin in ½ cup cold water. In a saucepan over medium heat, bring sugar, water, vinegar, and salt to a boil; combine with soaked gelatin. Mix celery, olives, pecans, pimentos, asparagus, and onion in Pyrex dish. Pour gelatin mixture over asparagus. Chill until set.

Virginia Robertson, Albany, GA

MCCALL'S PLANTATION SHRIMP SALAD
McCall played a big part in the opening of The Lady & Sons restaurant.
She remains very dear to our family.

2	tablespoons (more or less to taste) Old Bay Shrimp Boil	½	cup chopped onion
		½	cup chopped green olives
2	pounds shrimp, cleaned, peeled, and deveined		Pepper to taste
		1	cup mayonnaise
1	cup uncooked white rice		

Dissolve shrimp boil in 4 cups water and bring to a boil. Add shrimp and boil 4 minutes; drain, reserving shrimp boil water. Chop shrimp into bite-size chunks and put on paper towels; set aside to cool. In the reserved water, boil rice until tender for 15 to 20 minutes; drain rice in colander. Let cool. Add onion, olives, and pepper to rice; stir in mayonnaise. Add cooled, dry shrimp last.

McCall Holmes, Savannah, GA

ASIAN CHICKEN SALAD

*Jill is more of a sister to me than a sister-in-law. We are blessed
to have her in our family. She is a wonderful cook and has shared
many of her recipes with us.*

4	chicken breasts, cooked, diced	1	teaspoon freshly grated ginger
1½	cups bean sprouts	⅛	teaspoon salt
1½	cups snow peas	⅛	teaspoon sugar
¼	cup chopped scallions	½	cup chopped celery
¼	cup vegetable oil	1	8-ounce can sliced water
5	teaspoons soy sauce		chestnuts, drained

Combine chicken, bean sprouts, snow peas,
and scallions. Make marinade using oil, soy
sauce, ginger, salt, and sugar; add to chicken
mixture. Add celery and water chestnuts.
Serve chilled.   *Jill Hiers, Albany, GA*

Thank God for Jill!
She finally gave me
the girl I wanted
so badly—my niece
Corrie Hiers.

FROZEN FRUIT SALAD
WITH PINEAPPLE DRESSING

1	3-ounce package cream cheese, at room temperature	1	small can crushed pineapple, drained, juice reserved
3	tablespoons mayonnaise		Maraschino cherries, drained,
3	tablespoons honey		as many as you like
		½	pint whipping cream, whipped

Mix cream cheese and mayonnaise; add honey. Fold in fruit, then whipped
cream. Pour into ice cube tray and freeze. Makes 28 cubes. Serve with
Pineapple Dressing.

Pineapple Dressing

2	eggs, beaten	½	cup pineapple juice
⅓	cup honey		Dash of salt
1	tablespoon lemon juice	½	pint whipping cream, whipped

Combine all ingredients except whipped cream. Cook over low heat,
stirring until thick. Remove from heat, let cool for 20 minutes, then fold in
whipped cream. Serve spooned over squares of Frozen Fruit Salad.

Virginia Robertson, Albany, GA

FRENCH CREAM

1 8-ounce package cream cheese	¼ cup granulated sugar
1 cup powdered sugar	Juice and zest of 1 lemon
1 cup whipping cream	Pineapple juice

Soften cream cheese and then whip with powdered sugar until soft peaks form. In a separate bowl, whip together whipping cream and granulated sugar. Combine beaten cream cheese, sweetened whipped cream, lemon juice, and lemon zest; continue to beat, adding just enough pineapple juice to achieve desired consistency. Serve with fresh fruit salad. *the lady*

ROQUEFORT CREAM DRESSING

Trina was my mother's baby sister. She was only three years older than I was, and we were reared more as sisters than aunt and niece. We created much mischief as youngsters while the adults in our family were taking care of the motel, restaurant, and recreation center at River Bend in Albany, Georgia.

½ cup crumbled Roquefort cheese	1 tablespoon lemon juice
1 3-ounce package cream cheese, softened	1 tablespoon wine vinegar
½ cup mayonnaise	½ cup sour cream

Blend Roquefort and cream cheese until smooth. Mix in remaining ingredients. Beat well. Chill for 2 hours. Serve with vegetable crudité.

Aunt Trina Bearden, Houma, LA

BUTTERMILK DRESSING

½ cup sour cream	1 teaspoon House Seasoning
1 cup mayonnaise	2 tablespoons minced fresh parsley
½ cup buttermilk	1 tablespoon minced onion

Mix ingredients together and chill overnight. *the lady*

PASTA SALAD DRESSING

1   cup wine vinegar
⅔   cup oil
½   cup mayonnaise

1   package Good Seasons cheese
     Italian dressing mix
3   tablespoons sugar

Also good on spinach salad.

the lady

SWEET-AND-SOUR DRESSING

1½ cups vegetable oil
¾   cup vinegar
¾   cup sugar
1½ teaspoons salt

1½ teaspoons celery seed
1½ teaspoons dry mustard
1½ teaspoons paprika
1½ teaspoons grated onion

Combine all ingredients in a jar. Chill. Shake and serve over salad.
Kelley Ort, Atlanta, GA

POPPY SEED DRESSING

⅓   cup honey
¼   cup red wine vinegar
1   tablespoon Dijon mustard
1   tablespoon minced onion

1   teaspoon House Seasoning
1   tablespoon poppy seeds
¾   cup olive oil

Combine ingredients except oil in a blender. Process on low, gradually adding oil. Chill; shake or stir before serving.

the lady

HONEY MUSTARD DRESSING

¾ cup mayonnaise
3 tablespoons honey
1 tablespoon lemon juice or juice
   from ½ lemon

2 tablespoons yellow mustard
   Horseradish to taste
2 tablespoons orange juice
   (more or less as needed)

Combine all ingredients except orange juice; stir well. Thin to pouring consistency with orange juice. Cover and chill for 2 to 3 hours. Yields 1¼ cups.

the Lady

PEGGY'S ITALIAN DRESSING

Everybody loves my Aunt Peggy's dressing. She takes this basic recipe and changes it by using different condiments: mayonnaise, ketchup, etc.

4 cloves garlic, minced
½ teaspoon salt, or to taste
⅛ teaspoon pepper
¼ teaspoon dried basil
¼ teaspoon dried oregano
½ teaspoon paprika
⅛ teaspoon dried dill

   Pinch of dill seed
½ teaspoon sugar
½ teaspoon grated
   Parmesan cheese
1 teaspoon lemon juice
1¾ cups vinegar
¾ cup olive oil

Combine all ingredients and mix well.

Peggy Ort, Albany, GA

✔ Aunt Peggy has been my biggest supporter, spending weeks working with me, I was so busy. The memory of Aunt Peggy walking into my kitchen with clean cotton underpants on her head to keep her hair from falling into my food always brings a smile to my face. The women in my family are from the school of always make do.

Main Dishes & Seafood

BOURBON BEEF TENDERLOIN

*This recipe is for the grill. Beef can also be cooked in the oven at
350 degrees for 45 minutes to 1 hour. Use a meat thermometer:
rare—115 to 120 degrees; medium rare—130 to 135 degrees;
medium—140 to 145 degrees. The tenderloin, also called the fillet
of beef, is one of the most expensive cuts of beef, so you might want to
save this dish for a special occasion. Buy a whole tenderloin, about 4½
to 5 pounds, and have the butcher remove the "silver" connective tissue.*

1 cup bourbon	2 cups water
1 cup brown sugar	3 to 4 sprigs fresh thyme, chopped
⅔ cup soy sauce	1 beef tenderloin, silver
1 bunch cilantro, chopped	connective tissue removed
½ cup lemon juice	Oil for grill
1 tablespoon Worcestershire sauce	

Prepare marinade by combining bourbon, brown sugar, soy sauce, cilantro,
lemon juice, Worcestershire sauce, water, and thyme. Be sure tenderloin
is completely trimmed of any fat and connective tissue. Fold the tail end
of the beef back underneath itself so that it is of uniform thickness. Secure
with butcher's string. Pour marinade over meat, cover, and refrigerate 8 to
12 hours. Turn meat over several times during that time. Prepare grill for
cooking (or preheat oven to 350 degrees). When fire is ready, place meat
on oiled grill, reserving marinade. Cook over high heat with lid closed,
turning often; occasionally baste. Cooks rare in about 30 or 45 minutes in
the oven. Serve with Horseradish Cream on the side.

Horseradish Cream

1 cup heavy cream   ¼ cup horseradish, drained

Whip cream until stiff. Stir in horseradish, mixing well.

Kelley Ort, Atlanta, GA

32

SAUSAGE AND GRITS

1	cup uncooked grits	2	eggs, beaten
1	pound ground sausage	2	cups grated Cheddar cheese
1	onion, chopped	10	dashes Tabasco
2	4½-ounce cans green chilies, chopped	1	teaspoon paprika
1	stick butter	¼	cup chopped fresh parsley

Preheat oven to 325 degrees. Cook grits in 4 cups salted water until thick. Sauté sausage, breaking it into small pieces. Sauté onion in sausage fat; drain. Add onion and chilies to sausage. Add butter, eggs, cheese, and Tabasco to grits. Combine grits mixture with sausage mixture. Pour into a 13×9-inch casserole dish and garnish with additional small amounts of cheese, chilies, paprika, and parsley. Bake for 1 hour. Can be refrigerated up to 2 days before baking. Freezes well. Serves 10.

Jean Gregory, Brunswick, GA

SOUTHWESTERN BREAKFAST

Bacon	Refried beans
Potatoes (home fries)	Tortillas
Eggs	Cheese

Amounts determined by number of servings.

Cook bacon; reserve drippings. Cut potatoes in thin wedges and cook in bacon grease until soft and toasty; break eggs into potatoes and stir until eggs are scrambled. Heat refried beans. Layer each mixture on hot tortilla and top with cheese. Bake 1 minute to melt cheese.

Tara Bertram, Savannah, GA

CHICKEN BRUNSWICK STEW

1   2½-pound fryer
1   28-ounce can crushed tomatoes,
    sweetened with ⅓ cup sugar
1   16-ounce can creamed corn
1   cup ketchup
½   cup prepared barbecue sauce
1   onion, chopped

1   tablespoon liquid smoke
    (available in a bottle at
    grocery store)
1   tablespoon vinegar
1   tablespoon Worcestershire sauce
    Salt and pepper to taste
    Celery salt to taste

In a large pot, boil chicken until meat falls off bone, approximately
45 minutes; drain (reserve 1 to 2 cups of stock). Remove skin and bones;
chop meat. In a separate pot, mix chicken and remaining ingredients.
Simmer slowly for about 30 minutes, stirring often to prevent sticking.
(Add a little bit of stock if stew gets too thick.) Serve over steamed rice.

the Lady

SHRIMP PASTA CASSEROLE

2   eggs
1½ cups half-and-half
1   cup plain yogurt
½   cup grated Swiss cheese
⅓   cup crumbled feta cheese
⅓   cup chopped fresh parsley
1   teaspoon dried basil, crushed

1   teaspoon dried oregano, crushed
9   ounces angel hair pasta, cooked
16 ounces mild salsa, thick and
    chunky
2   pounds shrimp, cleaned, peeled,
    and deveined
½   cup grated Monterey Jack cheese

Preheat oven to 350 degrees. Grease a 12×8-inch pan or glass dish with
butter. Combine eggs, half-and-half, yogurt, Swiss and feta cheeses,
parsley, basil, and oregano in medium bowl; mix well. Spread half the
pasta on bottom of prepared pan. Cover with salsa. Add half of the shrimp.
Cover with Monterey Jack cheese. Cover with remaining pasta and shrimp.
Spread egg mixture over top. Bake for 30 minutes or until bubbly. Let
stand for 10 minutes.   *Kelley Ort, Atlanta, GA*

SAVANNAH BREAKFAST CASSEROLE

1 small onion, chopped	4 cups milk
1 bell pepper, chopped	½ teaspoon salt
½ cup chopped mushrooms	1½ teaspoons dry mustard
1 pound sausage	Black pepper to taste
8 slices bacon	Cayenne pepper to taste
9 eggs, beaten	½ cup Parmesan cheese
1½ cups grated cheese	8 slices white bread, cubed

Preheat oven to 350 degrees. Sauté onion, bell pepper, and mushrooms for just a minute; let cool. Scramble sausage and bacon until half-cooked; set aside. Mix eggs, cheese, milk, salt, dry mustard, black and cayenne peppers, Parmesan cheese, and cubed bread; add cooled onion mixture and ½ of the bacon mixture. Pour into greased casserole dish. Place remaining bacon and sausage mixture on top. Should be refrigerated overnight. Bake at 350 degrees uncovered for 45 to 60 minutes, or until center is cooked.

FOOLPROOF STANDING RIB ROAST

1 5-pound standing rib roast	1 tablespoon House Seasoning

Follow this method for a rib roast that is lusciously browned on the outside and rare on the inside—regardless of size. Allow roast to stand at room temperature for at least 1 hour. If roast is frozen, thaw completely; bring to room temperature. Preheat oven to 375 degrees. Rub roast with House Seasoning; place roast on rack in pan—rib side down, fatty side up. Roast for 1 hour. Turn off oven. Leave roast in oven but *do not open oven door*. Thirty to 40 minutes before serving time, turn oven to 375 degrees and reheat roast. *Important:* Do not remove roast or open oven door from time roast is put in until ready to serve.   *Anne S. Hanson, Albany, GA*

MOTHER'S "FARMERS' PORK CHOPS"

8	medium potatoes	1	cup all-purpose flour
½	medium onion	2	tablespoons Lawry's Seasoned Salt
	Salt and pepper to taste	8	center-cut pork chops, about
	White sauce (see recipe		½ inch thick
	below, or use your own)	⅓	cup vegetable oil

Preheat oven to 350 degrees. Peel potatoes; slice ¼ inch thick and cover with cold water. Slice onion into very thin slices. Cut slices in half. Drain potatoes; layer half the potatoes in a well-greased 15×10-inch casserole dish. Sprinkle with salt and pepper to taste. Scatter half of onion slices on top of potatoes. Repeat with remaining potatoes and onions. Cover potatoes with white sauce. Cover casserole dish with plastic wrap and microwave for 5 minutes on high or bake uncovered for 15 minutes. Mix together flour and seasoned salt and dredge pork chops in flour mixture. Lightly brown chops in vegetable oil. *Do not cook them completely.* As chops are removed from frying pan, lay them on top of potatoes. Bake at 350 degrees for 45 to 60 minutes. The juices from the pork chops will drip down into the potatoes. Delicious!

White Sauce

1	stick butter	4	cups milk
½	cup all-purpose flour	¼	cup chopped fresh parsley
1 to 2 teaspoons salt			or chives (optional)
½ to ¾ teaspoon pepper			

Melt butter; remove from heat. Stir in flour; add salt and pepper. Return to heat and cook, stirring constantly, until mixture is bubbly. Add milk, 1 cup at a time. Bring to a boil over medium heat, stirring frequently. Reduce heat and simmer 1 to 2 minutes, then let stand at least 1 to 2 minutes. Stir in parsley or chives, if desired.

Jeannene Powers, Albany, GA

MARYLAND CRAB CAKES

1	pound crabmeat, picked free of shell	1	teaspoon Worcestershire sauce
½	cup crushed Ritz crackers	1	teaspoon dry mustard
3	green onions, finely chopped, with tops		Juice of ½ lemon
½	cup finely chopped bell pepper	¼	teaspoon garlic powder
¼	cup mayonnaise	1	teaspoon salt
1	egg		Dash of cayenne pepper
			Flour for dusting
		½	cup peanut oil

Mix all ingredients together except flour and peanut oil. Shape into patties and dust with flour. Panfry in hot peanut oil over medium heat until browned, for 4 to 5 minutes. Flip and panfry other side until golden brown.

SHRIMP AND SCALLOP FRAÎCHE

½	cup crème fraîche	3	cloves garlic, minced
1	pound shrimp, cleaned, peeled, and deveined	1	tablespoon cognac or wine
1	pound fresh sea scallops	1	tablespoon cornstarch
½	stick butter	2	tablespoons fish or chicken stock
	Juice of 1 lemon	4	sprigs fresh basil

Crème Fraîche

1	cup heavy cream	2	tablespoons sour cream

Prepare crème fraîche ahead of time by combining heavy cream and sour cream. Cover with plastic wrap and let stand at room temperature for 12 to 24 hours. Clean and devein shrimp, leaving tails on. Pat scallops dry with paper towels. Melt butter in a large skillet. Add lemon juice and garlic. Place shrimp and scallops in butter and sauté until scallops are opaque, 3 to 4 minutes per side. Remove to a warm platter. Add cognac or wine to pan juice. Dissolve cornstarch in stock and add along with crème fraîche to pan. Simmer until thickened. Pour sauce over shellfish and garnish with basil sprigs.

Kelley Ort, Atlanta, GA

SCALLOPS CHARLESTON

1½ pounds fresh sea scallops
 Salt and pepper to taste
½ teaspoon garlic powder
¼ teaspoon paprika
¼ cup finely chopped fresh basil
 Flour for dusting
¾ cup sherry or dry white wine

1 shallot, finely chopped
8 ounces fresh mushrooms,
 quartered
2 tablespoons butter
3 tablespoons all-purpose flour
1 cup grated Gruyère cheese

Season scallops with salt, pepper, garlic powder, paprika, and basil.
Dust scallops with flour. Sauté in a pan that has been lightly coated with
nonstick cooking spray and a small amount of olive oil. Cook scallops on
both sides until browned. Remove scallops from pan. To the drippings in
the pan, add sherry, shallots, and mushrooms; cook for approximately 3 to
4 minutes. In a separate saucepan, melt butter over medium heat and add
3 tablespoons flour. Mix well and cook for 2 minutes over low heat,
stirring constantly. Pour shallots, mushrooms, and liquid from scallops into
flour mixture. Mix well. Stir scallops into sauce. (If too thick, you can thin
with clam juice or fish or chicken stock.) Transfer to four individual baking
dishes, top with cheese, and broil for 1 minute, until browned. Serve
with wild rice.

the lady

SHRIMP BISQUE

*Today, Carolyn and I share recipes and time together when we can.
She is the daughter of Hugh and Bernice Crum, who were very close
friends of my parents. While growing up, Carolyn and I enjoyed many
meals that our mothers prepared together.*

1 10¾-ounce can condensed
 cream of mushroom soup
1 10¾-ounce can condensed
 cream of chicken soup
2 12-ounce cans evaporated milk
2 tablespoons butter

½ pound cooked shrimp, peeled,
 deveined, and chopped
 Dash of Worcestershire sauce
 Dash of Tabasco
¼ cup sherry, or to taste

In top of double boiler, heat soups, milk, and butter over boiling water.
Add shrimp, Worcestershire sauce, and Tabasco. Stir in sherry to taste.
Continue heating until desired temperature. Great served plain or over
steamed rice.   *Carolyn Cundiff, Athens, GA*

CRAB BISQUE

Susan is a dear person. On more than one occasion, I have had the
pleasure of her joining me in the kitchen preparing The Bag Lady meals.

1	10¾-ounce can cream of asparagus soup	¼	cup half-and-half
1	10¾-ounce can cream of mushroom soup	½	pound crabmeat, picked free of shell
¼	cup milk	¼	cup dry sherry

In a heavy saucepan, combine all ingredients and bring to a boil. Reduce
heat and simmer for 5 minutes. This delicate-tasting soup can be frozen for
up to 1 month. Serves 4.   *Susan Williams, Albany, GA*

HUNGARIAN CHICKEN PAPRIKA

1	large onion, chopped	2	teaspoons salt
1	clove garlic, minced	1½	cups water
4	tablespoons olive oil	1	cup sour cream
1	4- to 5-pound chicken, cut up	1	tablespoon all-purpose flour
2	tablespoons paprika		Dumplings (optional)
1	teaspoon pepper		

In a deep skillet over medium heat, brown onion and garlic in oil. Add
chicken and brown on all sides, about 10 minutes. Sprinkle paprika,
pepper, and salt on chicken. Turn meat once. Add water, cover, and simmer
on low heat for approximately 30 minutes or until meat is tender. Remove
from liquid. In a small bowl, mix sour cream, flour, and 1 cup of hot
liquid from chicken until smooth. Pour mixture into skillet and blend with
remaining liquid. Add dumplings if desired and heat through. This dish
may be served over noodles or rice instead of dumplings.

Dumplings

3	eggs, beaten	1	teaspoon salt
3	cups all-purpose flour	½	cup water

Blend all ingredients and mix well. Drop batter by teaspoonfuls into
boiling water. Cook about 10 minutes and drain. Rinse with cold water and
drain again.   *Pat Andres, Savannah, GA*

CHICKEN AND DUMPLINGS

1	2½-pound chicken	1	teaspoon House Seasoning
3	ribs celery, chopped	4	quarts water
1	large onion, chopped	1	10¾-ounce can condensed
2	bay leaves		cream of celery or cream of
2	chicken bouillon cubes		chicken soup

Cut up chicken, but do not remove skin. The skin and bones can be removed later. Place chicken, celery, onion, bay leaves, bouillon, and House Seasoning in water and boil at a rolling boil for 30 to 45 minutes, until meat begins to fall off the bones. Remove skin and bones at this point, along with bay leaves. Return chicken to pan. Prepare dumplings and set them aside for a few minutes. Add cream soup to chicken and continue to boil. If desired, you can thicken the stock a little by mixing 2 tablespoons cornstarch with ¼ cup of water and adding it to the stock. Drop dumplings into boiling stock. Never stir dumplings. Shake the pot gently in a circular motion to submerge dumplings in stock. Cook for a few minutes more, until dumplings are done. Do not overcook.

Dumplings

2	cups all-purpose flour mixed with 1 teaspoon salt	¾	cup ice water

Put flour in a mixing bowl. Beginning in center of flour, dribble small amount of ice water. Work mixture with fingers from center of bowl to sides of bowl, incorporating small amounts of water at a time. Continue until all flour is used up. Batter will feel as if it is going to be tough. Knead dough and form into ball. Dust a good amount of flour onto dough board and rolling pin. Roll out dough, working from center. Dough will be firm. Roll to ⅛ inch thinness. Let it air-dry for a minute or two while you return your attention to the boiling pot at the point at which you add the canned soup to the chicken mixture. Cut dumplings into 1-inch strips. Working with one strip at a time, hold strip over pot, pull it in half, and drop into the boiling stock. Remember, do not stir mixture after dumplings have been added to pot. *Hint:* Frozen dumplings are available in most supermarkets if you don't have the time to make them.

the Lady

MEXICAN CHICKEN

1   10¾-ounce can cream of
    chicken soup
1   10¾-ounce can Cheddar
    cheese soup
1   10¾-ounce can cream of
    mushroom soup

1   10-ounce can Ro-Tel tomatoes
1   whole chicken, cooked, boned,
    and chopped, or 4 cups leftover
    cooked chicken
1   11½-ounce package flour tortillas
2   cups shredded Cheddar cheese

In a large bowl, stir together soups and tomatoes. Stir in chicken. In a
greased 13×9-inch pan, layer tortillas and chicken mixture, beginning and
ending with tortillas. Sprinkle Cheddar cheese over casserole, and bake at
350 degrees for 30 minutes.   *Carolyn Cundiff, Athens, GA*

CHICKEN IN WINE SAUCE

4   large skinless boneless chicken
    breasts
6   ounces Swiss cheese slices
1   10¾-ounce can condensed
    cream of chicken soup

¼   cup white wine (more if desired)
    Salt and pepper to taste
1   cup herb-flavored Pepperidge
    Farm stuffing mix, crushed
½   stick butter, melted

Preheat oven to 350 degrees. Place chicken in shallow buttered casserole.
Layer cheese on top. Mix soup, wine, salt, and pepper; pour over cheese.
Sprinkle stuffing mix on top and drizzle with melted butter. Bake for 45 to
60 minutes.   *Claire Watts, Savannah, GA*

THE LADY'S CHEESY MAC

4   cups cooked elbow macaroni,
    drained (approximately 2 cups
    uncooked)
2   cups grated Cheddar cheese
3   eggs, beaten

½   cup sour cream
½   stick butter, cut into pieces
½   teaspoon salt
1   cup milk, or equivalent in
    evaporated milk

Preheat oven to 350 degrees. After macaroni has been boiled and drained,
add Cheddar cheese while macaroni is still hot. Combine remaining
ingredients and add to macaroni mixture. Pour into casserole dish and bake
for 30 to 45 minutes. Top with additional cheese, if desired.   *the lady*

CHEESEBURGER MEAT LOAF WITH CHEESE SAUCE

2   pounds ground beef
2   teaspoons House Seasoning
1   medium onion, chopped
1   medium bell pepper, chopped
1   cup grated Cheddar cheese
¼   cup Worcestershire sauce
1   cup sour cream
1   cup crushed Ritz crackers
1   teaspoon Lawry's Seasoned Salt
8 to 10 slices white bread

Preheat oven to 325 degrees. Mix all ingredients except bread slices well. Shape into loaf. Place loaf on 1-inch-deep jelly roll pan lined with white bread slices. Bake loaf for 45 to 60 minutes. The bread absorbs the grease and should be discarded after loaf is removed from oven. Serves 6 to 8.

the lady

Cheese Sauce

1   10¾-ounce can condensed cream of mushroom soup
1   soup-can measure of milk
1½ cups grated Cheddar cheese

Heat soup and milk over medium heat; add cheese. Pour over meat loaf or pass at the table.

the lady

MARJORIE'S MEAT LOAF

Anne and I have been friends since high school, and she has a wonderful sense of humor. She is also a very good cook. Susan, Anne, and I have shared years of food and fun together.

1½ pounds ground beef
½   pound ground pork or hot sausage
1   cup seasoned bread crumbs
⅓   cup milk
⅓   cup relish
3   eggs
1   cup Cheddar cheese, cubed

Topping

8   ounces tomato sauce
2   tablespoons chopped onion
2   tablespoons relish
1   tablespoon vinegar
3   tablespoons brown sugar
⅓   cup catsup

Combine meat loaf ingredients; shape into two loaves. Combine topping ingredients; pour over loaves. Bake at 350 degrees for 1½ hours. One loaf can be frozen for later use.

Anne S. Hanson, Albany, GA

SWISS STEAK

1	round steak (approximately 1½ pounds)	⅓	cup vegetable oil
1	teaspoon garlic powder	2	cloves garlic, crushed
	Salt and pepper to taste	1	14½-ounce can diced tomatoes
	Flour for dusting	1	medium onion, cut into strips
		1	medium bell pepper, cut into strips

Cut steak into serving-size pieces. Season to taste with garlic powder and salt and pepper. Dust meat with flour. In heavy skillet, brown both sides of meat in vegetable oil. Transfer to Dutch oven. Combine garlic, tomatoes, onion, bell pepper, and 1 tomato-can measure of water. Pour over steak and simmer until meat is tender. Season to taste with additional salt and pepper. *Hint:* This is good to cook in Crock-Pot on low for a most fabulous dinner.

THE LADY'S OXTAILS

2 to 3 pounds oxtails		1	bell pepper, cut in strips
	House Seasoning to taste	3	bay leaves
	Lawry's Seasoned Salt	½	cup Worcestershire sauce
1	large onion, cut in strips		

Wash and season meat to taste with a mixture of House Seasoning and Lawry's Seasoned Salt. Place all ingredients in covered casserole and bake in slow oven at 300 degrees for 3 to 4 hours. Check after 2½ hours: the meat is done when it begins to fall off the bone. After oxtails are done, thicken sauce with mixture of 2 tablespoons cornstarch in ¼ cup water.

PECAN CHICKEN

1	stick butter	1	tablespoon paprika
1	cup buttermilk	⅛	teaspoon pepper
1	egg, lightly beaten	¼	cup sesame seeds
1	cup all-purpose flour	2	2½-pound chickens, cut into
1	cup ground pecans		quarters or pieces
1	tablespoon salt	¼	cup pecan halves

Preheat oven to 350 degrees. Melt butter in a 10×15-inch baking pan. In a shallow dish, combine buttermilk and egg. In another dish combine flour, pecans, salt, paprika, pepper, and sesame seeds. Dip chicken in buttermilk, then in flour. Place skin side down in melted butter. Turn to coat and leave skin side up. Sprinkle with pecan halves. Bake for 1¼ hours.

Anne S. Hanson, Albany, GA

COOKIE'S HOMEMADE CRAB STEW

Never would I have thought too much butter was bad, but the original recipe called for 1 pound of butter, which was way too much. I have adjusted the amount to ½ cup.

2	medium onions, diced	1	pound thin bacon, fried crisp, crumbled
½	cup butter	½	gallon whole milk
1	pound crab meat		Salt and pepper to taste

Sauté onions with ½ of the butter until tender. Add crab to onion mixture, cook on medium heat for 10 minutes. Add bacon, milk, remaining butter, and salt and pepper; heat until soft boil. Serve hot.

Mary Hill, Savannah, GA

SHRIMP OR LOBSTER BISQUE

8 ounces cooked shrimp or lobster meat
2 tablespoons sherry, plus additional to taste
Pinch of thyme
3 to 4 green onions with tops, chopped
2 tablespoons butter

1 10¾-ounce can condensed tomato soup
1 soup-can measure of milk
1 10¾-ounce can condensed cream of mushroom soup
1 soup-can measure of heavy cream
Chopped fresh parsley, for garnish

Finely chop the shrimp or lobster meat and marinate 30 minutes in 2 tablespoons of sherry and the thyme. Sauté onions in butter until soft. Add shrimp or lobster meat and cook over a low heat for 3 to 5 minutes. In a separate bowl, combine tomato soup with milk and blend mushroom soup with cream. Combine the two soup mixtures with the shrimp-lobster sauté. Simmer over low heat for 3 to 5 minutes. Add more sherry to taste. Cool, then mix in blender until thick and smooth. To serve, reheat in a double boiler. Add more sherry to taste and garnish with chopped parsley.

Kelley Ort, Atlanta, GA

BRENDA'S STEAK 'N' GRAVY

1½ pounds stew meat
2 tablespoons butter
2 tablespoons flour
½ cup water
2 10¾-ounce cans golden mushroom soup

1 8-ounce bag egg noodles, prepared according to package directions

In a heavy skillet, over medium heat, brown all sides of stew meat. Remove from heat; place meat in Crock-Pot. Use drippings in skillet to make gravy: add butter and flour and brown, then stir in water. Add soup. Stir and cook for 5 minutes. Pour over meat in slow cooker. Cook on low setting for 6 to 8 hours. Serve over cooked noodles.

Brenda Tucker, Jacksonville, FL

SHRIMP WITH RICE

2 6-ounce boxes Uncle Ben's
  long-grain and wild rice
2 pounds shrimp, cleaned, peeled,
  and deveined
1 onion, diced and sautéed in
  2 tablespoons butter
1 bell pepper, chopped

2 10¾-ounce cans condensed
  cream of mushroom soup
16 ounces grated Cheddar cheese;
  reserve ½ cup for top
1 tablespoon Worcestershire
  sauce
½ teaspoon dry mustard

Remove seasoning mix from rice; do not use. Cook rice as directed on
box. Preheat oven to 375 degrees. Mix rice with remaining ingredients in
a baking dish and sprinkle reserved cheese on top. Bake for 45 minutes.

Jacklyn Miller, Guyton, GA

DOT'S CHICKEN AND RICE

*Dot was one of my first customers when I started The Lady Restaurant.
She has been one of my biggest supporters. Thanks so much, Dot.*

3 cups diced cooked chicken
1 medium onion, diced and sautéed
1 8-ounce can water chestnuts,
  drained and chopped
2 14½-ounce cans French green
  beans, rinsed and drained
1 4-ounce can pimentos, rinsed
  and drained

1 10¾-ounce can condensed
  cream of celery soup
1 cup mayonnaise
1 6-ounce box Uncle Ben's long-
  grain and wild rice, cooked
  according to package directions
1 cup grated sharp Cheddar cheese

Preheat oven to 300 degrees. Mix all ingredients together and pour into a
3-quart casserole. Bake for 25 minutes.

Mrs. Linton H. Smith Jr., Savannah, GA

BARBECUE MEAT LOAF

1½	pounds ground beef	2	8-ounce cans tomato sauce
1	cup fresh breadcrumbs	½	cup water
1	onion, chopped	3	tablespoons vinegar
1	egg, lightly beaten	3	tablespoons brown sugar
1½	teaspoons salt	2	tablespoons prepared mustard
½	teaspoon pepper	2	tablespoons Worcestershire sauce

Mix together beef, breadcrumbs, onion, egg, salt, pepper, and ½ cup of the tomato sauce. Form mixture into a loaf and place in a shallow pan. Stir together remaining tomato sauce, water, vinegar, brown sugar, mustard, and Worcestershire sauce. Pour sauce over meat loaf. Bake at 350 degrees for 1 hour, basting occasionally with pan juices.

Jacklyn Miller, Guyton, GA

HOT CHICKEN SALAD

2	cups cooked chicken, diced	½	cup salad dressing
1	cup chopped celery		Pimentos
1	cup blanched almonds	¾	cup crushed potato chips
2	hard-boiled eggs	½	cup grated American cheese
1	tablespoon onion salt		

Mix all but chips and cheese and place in a greased baking dish. Top with potato chips and American cheese. Bake at 350 degrees for 30 minutes.

Alberta DiClaudio, Savannah, GA

PIGGY PUDDING

16	link pork sausages	1	7½-ounce package corn bread
4 to 5 tart apples, peeled, cored,			mix (prepare batter according
	and sliced		to directions on package)

Preheat oven to 450 degrees. Cook sausages until done, piercing with fork to let out fat. Drain, then arrange in a 9-inch square baking dish. Layer sliced apples on top. Pour corn bread batter over all and bake for approximately 30 minutes or until corn bread is done. Serve with warm maple syrup. Serves 4 to 5. *Diane Silver Berryhill, Savannah, GA*

CHILI-CHICKEN

½ cup chopped onion
2 tablespoons butter
3 cans mushroom soup
   Salt and pepper to taste
1 4-ounce can pimentos, chopped

2 tablespoons chopped green chilies
2 or 3 cups grated sharp cheese
16 ounces noodles, cooked
4 cups cooked and cubed chicken

Sauté onion in butter; stir in soup, salt, pepper, pimentos, and green chilies. Add cheese, reserving small amount to sprinkle on top. Spray bottom and sides of 4-quart casserole. Layer noodles, chicken, and soup mixture and sprinkle top with remaining cheese. Bake at 350 degrees for 45 minutes.

Sheila Mims, Albany, GA

BEEF ROAST

1 eye of round roast (be sure you know exact weight)
½ cup red Burgundy wine

⅓ cup soy sauce
2 tablespoons cracked black pepper

Place roast in glass container large enough to hold it comfortably. Make marinade of Burgundy wine, soy sauce, and pepper. Pour over meat and marinate overnight. Next day, place roast in shallow pan with just a little of the marinade. Preheat oven to 500 degrees. Cook uncovered for 5 minutes per pound of meat. Turn off oven and cover roast with foil. Leave in oven for 40 minutes for medium-rare roast. Let cool and slice very thin. *the lady*

SPECIAL OCCASION CHICKEN

½ stick butter
4 skinless boneless chicken breast halves
1 cup sliced fresh mushrooms

2 tablespoons minced shallots
¼ teaspoon salt
¼ teaspoon pepper
4 ounces grated mozzarella cheese

Melt butter over medium heat. Add mushrooms and shallots and sprinkle with salt and pepper. Cook 10 minutes. Add chicken and cook 10 minutes on each side, or until tender. Transfer chicken to platter and sprinkle with grated cheese. Top with mushroom mixture. Cover and let stand 5 minutes or until cheese melts. Serves 4 to 6. *Jill Hiers, Albany, GA*

CHICKEN CASSEROLE

1	fryer, cooked, boned, and cut into small pieces (reserve broth)	2½	cups chicken broth
½	cup mayonnaise	1	package Pepperidge Farm corn bread stuffing mix
½	cup chopped onion	1	cup milk
4	eggs	1	10¾-ounce can condensed cream of chicken soup
1	stick butter, melted		

Combine chicken, mayonnaise, and chopped onion and set aside. Combine 2 eggs, the butter, chicken broth, and corn bread stuffing mix and set aside. In small bowl, lightly beat 2 eggs and milk. Spray large casserole dish with nonstick cooking spray. In bottom of dish, spread half the stuffing mixture; then layer with chicken mixture. Add second layer of stuffing mixture. Pour egg and milk mixture over top layer of stuffing mixture. Refrigerate overnight. Preheat oven to 350 degrees. Spread cream of chicken soup on top of casserole and bake for 45 minutes.   *Sheila Mims, Albany, GA*

PEPPER STEAK

1	1½-pound round steak	1	large onion
	Sprinkle of paprika	1	large bell pepper
2	tablespoons butter	2	tablespoons cornstarch
	Garlic salt to taste	¼	cup water
1	10½-ounce can beef broth	¼	cup soy sauce

Pound round steak and cut into ¼-inch strips; sprinkle with paprika. Brown meat in butter; add garlic salt and beef broth. Cover; simmer for 30 minutes. Cut onion and pepper into strips. Add to meat and simmer for 5 minutes. Mix cornstarch, water, and soy sauce and add to meat mixture. Simmer until sauce thickens slightly. Serve over rice.

Denise Watson, Albany, GA

MEXICAN LASAGNA

Amy is the daughter of one of my best friends. "Little Itch" will always have a special place in my heart. I can't believe she's now a grown woman.

1½ pounds ground beef
1½ teaspoons ground cumin
1 tablespoon chili powder
¼ teaspoon garlic powder
¼ teaspoon cayenne pepper
   Salt and black pepper to taste
1 16-ounce can diced tomatoes
12 corn tortillas
2 cups small-curd cottage cheese

1 cup grated Monterey Jack
   cheese with peppers
1 egg
½ cup grated Cheddar cheese
2 cups shredded lettuce
½ cup chopped tomatoes
3 green onions, chopped
¼ cup sliced black olives

Brown ground beef; drain thoroughly. Add cumin, chili powder, garlic powder, cayenne pepper, salt and black pepper, and tomatoes; heat through. Cover bottom and sides of a 13×9×2-inch baking dish with tortillas. Pour beef mixture over tortillas; place a layer of tortillas over meat mixture and set aside. Combine cottage cheese, Monterey Jack cheese, and egg; pour over tortillas. Bake at 350 degrees for 30 minutes. Remove from oven; sprinkle rows of Cheddar cheese, lettuce, tomatoes, green onions, and olives diagonally across top of casserole.

Amy Dupuy, Albany, GA

SEAFOOD THERMIDOR

2 tablespoons butter
1 small onion or shallot, minced
8 ounces sliced fresh mushrooms
   Salt and black pepper to taste
2 pounds fresh lobster, scallops, or
   shrimp (or combination), cooked

1 10¾-ounce can Cheddar
   cheese soup
2 tablespoons pimentos
   Paprika, for sprinkling

In a sauté pan, melt butter over medium heat. Add onions and sauté for 3 minutes. Add mushrooms and season with salt and black pepper. Cook, stirring, for 5 minutes. Add seafood and cook for 2 to 3 minutes. Add cheese soup and stir for 2 more minutes. Stir in pimentos. Pour over hot buttered rice and sprinkle with paprika. Broil several minutes until golden brown.

Jill Hiers, Albany, GA

MUSHROOM-STUFFED BAKED RED SNAPPER

Suzette is the older sister of Amy. She will always have my undying admiration. "Go, girl!"

½ pound fresh mushrooms, or one 8-ounce can stems and pieces
½ stick butter
½ cup finely chopped celery
5 tablespoons minced onion
1 8-ounce can water chestnuts, drained and chopped
½ cup soft bread crumbs
1 egg, lightly beaten

1 tablespoon soy sauce
1 tablespoon chopped fresh parsley
Salt and pepper to taste
2 2½-pound oven-ready whole red snappers, gutted, scaled, and cleaned
½ cup dry white wine
¾ cup water

Preheat oven to 350 degrees. Rinse, pat dry, and finely chop ¼ pound mushrooms. Quarter remaining mushrooms or drain canned mushrooms. Set aside. In a small skillet, melt 2 tablespoons of the butter; add celery and 3 tablespoons of the onion. Sauté for 5 minutes. Combine sautéed celery mixture with mushrooms, water chestnuts, bread crumbs, egg, soy sauce, parsley, and salt and pepper. Mix well and spoon into fish cavities. Secure openings with skewers or toothpicks. Sprinkle both sides of each fish with salt and pepper. Place in a large baking dish. Dot with remaining 2 tablespoons of the butter, 2 tablespoons onion, the wine, and water. Bake uncovered for 45 to 50 minutes. Baste occasionally. Test with a fork. When fish flakes, it's done.

Amy and Suzette Dupuy's mother, Susan, and I were both expecting our first babies when we met. The "Sweet & Savory Sisters," Amy and Suzette, honor their mother and father by serving the best dang southern/Cajun meals at their restaurant Sass, in Thomasville, Georgia.

Suzette Dupuy Wagner, Albany, GA

CHICKEN ITALIAN

1   large onion, chopped
1   green pepper, chopped
2   cans tomato sauce
1   #2 can small English peas
1   small can mushrooms
1   5- to 6-pound hen, boiled,
    boned, chopped

1   tablespoon Worcestershire
    sauce
    Salt and pepper to taste
    Dash garlic salt
2   packages fine noodles,
    cooked in chicken broth

Make sauce of onions and bell pepper cooked in vegetable oil. Add tomato sauce; cook until thick. Add peas, mushrooms, chicken, and seasonings. Make nest of noodles on individual plates; put sauce in center. Serves 8 to 10.   *Virginia Robertson, Albany, GA*

DUCK BURGUNDY

4   whole ducks
    Salt and pepper to taste
    Garlic powder to taste
    Poultry seasoning to taste
1   large onion, quartered
1   apple, quartered

1   orange, quartered
4   ribs celery, cut into 1-inch
    pieces
⅓   cup soy sauce
⅓   cup vegetable oil
½   cup red Burgundy wine

Preheat oven to 450 degrees. Clean ducks well and rub body cavities lightly with salt, pepper, garlic powder, and poultry seasoning. Stuff cavities with pieces of onion, apple, orange, and celery. Rub ducks with soy sauce and oil. Place in baking pan. Roast uncovered, basting often with Burgundy wine. Allow 10 to 15 minutes baking time per pound of duck. Remove stuffing before serving.   *the lady*

CHICKEN POT PIE AND PASTRY

1	10¾-ounce can condensed Cheddar cheese soup	1	10-ounce package frozen green peas (or one 8-ounce can, drained)
1	10¾-ounce can condensed cream of celery soup	3	carrots, sliced, cooked, and drained
½	cup milk		Salt and pepper to taste
1	chicken, skinned, cooked, boned, and cubed	1	pastry for top and bottom
1	medium onion, diced		Butter to dot pastry

In a large saucepan, heat soups and milk. Stir in chicken, onion, peas, carrots, and salt and pepper. Cook until mixture boils. Remove from heat. Preheat oven to 350 degrees. Pour into a pastry-lined 13×9×2-inch pan. Cut pastry for top into strips. Lay over pie filling in a lattice style. Dot with butter. Bake for 45 minutes until golden brown.

Pastry

3	cups all-purpose flour	¾	cup Crisco shortening
1	teaspoon salt		Ice water
¼	teaspoon baking powder		

Sift together flour, salt, and baking powder. Cut in shortening with pastry blender until pieces are the size of small peas. Sprinkle 1 to 2 tablespoons of ice water over part of mixture. Gently toss with fork; push to side of bowl. Repeat until all is moistened. Form into 2 balls. Flatten each on a lightly floured surface by pressing with edge of hand three times across in both directions. With a floured rolling pin, roll out on floured surface. Roll from center to edge until ⅛ inch thick.

the lady

DEVILED SEAFOOD CASSEROLE

1½ pounds shrimp, cleaned, peeled, and deveined
1 pound fresh sea scallops
1½ sticks butter
1 1-pound haddock fillet
½ cup plus 1 tablespoon all-purpose flour
1 cup evaporated milk
1 cup consommé or beef broth
2 tablespoons cornstarch
⅓ cup milk
1 teaspoon garlic powder

1 tablespoon horseradish
½ teaspoon salt
1 teaspoon soy sauce
2 tablespoons chopped fresh parsley
1 tablespoon Worcestershire sauce
1 teaspoon dry mustard
¼ teaspoon cayenne pepper
1 tablespoon lemon juice
4 teaspoons ketchup
½ cup sherry

Preheat oven to 400 degrees. Sauté shrimp and scallops in 4 tablespoons of the butter for 3 to 5 minutes, until tender. In a saucepan, steam fish in small amount of water for 3 minutes, until tender, and cut into bite-size pieces. In a saucepan, melt remaining 8 tablespoons of the butter; add flour and evaporated milk; mix and add consommé. Cook over medium heat until thick. Mix cornstarch in ⅓ cup of milk and add remaining ingredients except sherry. Add to sauce and stir well. Add seafood and stir in sherry. Pour into a casserole and bake for 30 minutes. Serves 8.

Virginia Robertson, Albany, GA

OLD-TIME BEEF STEW

2 pounds stew beef	½ teaspoon pepper
2 tablespoons vegetable oil	½ teaspoon paprika
2 cups water	Dash of ground allspice
1 teaspoon Worcestershire sauce	or ground cloves
1 clove garlic, peeled	3 large carrots, sliced
1 or 2 bay leaves	4 red potatoes, quartered
1 medium onion, sliced	3 ribs celery, chopped
1 teaspoon salt	2 tablespoons cornstarch
1 teaspoon sugar	

Brown meat in hot oil. Add water, Worcestershire sauce, garlic, bay
leaves, onion, salt, sugar, pepper, paprika, and allspice. Cover and simmer
1½ hours. Remove bay leaves and garlic clove. Add carrots, potatoes, and
celery. Cover and cook 30 to 40 minutes longer. To thicken gravy, remove
2 cups hot liquid. Using a separate bowl, combine ¼ cup water and
cornstarch until smooth. Mix with hot liquid and return mixture to pot.
Stir and cook until bubbly. *Jill Hiers, Albany, GA*

LASAGNE

2 pounds ground beef	6 to 8 long strips lasagne noodles
2 cloves garlic	8 ounces sliced Swiss cheese
2 6-ounce cans tomato paste	¾ pound mozzarella cheese,
1 1-pound can tomatoes	crumbled
1 teaspoon salt	12 ounces cottage cheese
Dash of pepper	Parmesan cheese
1 teaspoon oregano	

Lightly grease a 3-quart casserole. Brown beef and garlic in a large
saucepan; add tomato paste, tomatoes, salt, pepper, and oregano; cover and
simmer 20 minutes. Cook noodles, drain, separate. In a casserole, layer
meat sauce, noodles, Swiss cheese, mozzarella cheese, and cottage cheese.
Repeat layers, ending with sauce. Dust with Parmesan cheese. Bake at
350 degrees for 20 to 30 minutes. Cuts better if it stands for 10 minutes.
Do not cook before freezing. Serves 8 to 10. *Jill Hiers, Albany, GA*

BAKED SPAGHETTI

2 large onions, chopped
1 medium green pepper, chopped
2 pounds ground beef
3 cans tomato soup
3 cans water
1 medium jar chopped black olives, juice reserved

6 tablespoons Worcestershire sauce
¾ pound grated cheese
2 small boxes spaghetti, cooked and drained
1 can mushroom soup
Salt and pepper to taste

In a medium skillet, sauté onions and green pepper. Add beef and brown. Add tomato soup, water, juice of olives, and Worcestershire sauce. Cook over medium heat until thick, about 1 to 2 hours. Add cheese, olives, and cooked spaghetti. Pour into greased casserole. Spread mushroom soup on top and season with salt and pepper. Bake at 350 degrees for 30 minutes. Serves 12.

Jill Hiers, Albany, GA

SESAME CHICKEN STRIPS

6 skinless boneless chicken breast halves
1 cup sour cream
1 tablespoon lemon juice, or juice of ½ lemon
2 teaspoons celery salt
2 teaspoons Worcestershire sauce

½ teaspoon salt
¼ teaspoon pepper
2 cloves garlic, minced
1 cup dry bread crumbs
⅓ cup sesame seeds
½ stick butter, melted

Lightly grease a 15×10-inch jelly roll pan. Cut chicken crosswise into ½-inch strips. In a large bowl, combine sour cream, lemon juice, celery salt, Worcestershire sauce, salt, pepper, and garlic. Mix well. Add chicken to mixture, coat well, and cover. Refrigerate at least 8 hours or overnight. Preheat oven to 350 degrees. In medium bowl, combine bread crumbs and sesame seeds. Remove chicken strips from sour cream mixture. Roll in crumb mixture, coating evenly. Arrange in single layer in prepared pan. Spoon butter evenly over chicken. Bake for 40 to 45 minutes or until chicken is tender and golden brown. Serve with honey mustard.

Nancy Blood, Savannah, GA

SOLE PAPRIKA

1½	pounds fillet of sole	1	tablespoon all-purpose flour
1	onion, sliced thin		Juice of ½ lemon
1	cup sour cream	½	teaspoon paprika
⅓	cup white table wine		Salt and pepper to taste

Preheat oven to 375 degrees. Arrange fillets in a greased shallow baking dish. Cover with onion slices. Blend sour cream, wine, flour, lemon juice, and seasonings and pour over entire baking dish. Bake for about 25 minutes, or until fish is tender. Serves 3 to 4.   *the lady*

MARINATED CORNISH HENS

2	split Cornish hens	1	bay leaf
1	onion, diced	¼	teaspoon dried thyme
1	clove garlic, minced	2	tablespoons sherry
1	stick butter		Salt and pepper to taste
1	10¾-ounce can beef broth	16	ounces fresh mushrooms, sliced

Wash, pat dry, and salt and pepper hens. Place in long, flat baking dish. Sauté onion and garlic in butter. Add remaining ingredients except the mushrooms. Stir and pour over hens; cover and refrigerate overnight. Preheat oven to 350 degrees. Add mushrooms and bake for 1 hour, basting frequently. Serve with wild rice. *Variation:* Chicken can be substituted for Cornish hens.   *Nancy Blood, Savannah, GA*

HAMBURGER CASSEROLE

1	pound hamburger meat	1	small potato
1	can mushroom soup	1	small onion

Brown hamburger meat and drain. Add soup and 1 can of water. Stir and simmer. While meat is simmering, thinly slice potato and onion. In casserole dish, alternate layers of meat, potato, and onion, ending with meat mixture. Bake at 350 degrees for 30 minutes.   *Denise Watson, Albany, GA*

HERB-BAKED CHICKEN

Shelly is the mother of Michael Peay, who is a server in our restaurant. Michael is a vital part of our business and one of Jamie and Bobby's closest friends. My sons have enjoyed many a good meal prepared by this lady.

1	1- to 2-pound chicken, cut in quarters, skin removed	¼	teaspoon dried rosemary
3 to 4	tablespoons olive oil	1	teaspoon chopped fresh ginger
¼	cup teriyaki sauce	½	teaspoon salt
¼	teaspoon dried oregano	⅛	teaspoon pepper
		1	lemon, sliced thin

Preheat oven to 350 degrees. Coat chicken with oil and place in baking dish. Sprinkle with teriyaki sauce. Combine oregano, rosemary, ginger, salt, and pepper; sprinkle over chicken. Top with lemon slices. Bake for about 1 hour.   *Shelly Peay, Richmond Hill, GA*

SPICY SAUSAGE AND VEGETABLE FRITTATA

Resa was kind enough to submit these through Nancy Blood. We have heard that Resa is a marvelous cook.

8	ounces hot Italian sausage, casings removed	1	green bell pepper, diced
1	medium zucchini, diced	6	eggs
1	red bell pepper, diced	4	ounces mozzarella cheese

Crumble sausage into a 10-inch nonstick skillet. Cook 2 to 3 minutes over medium heat until no pink remains. Add zucchini and peppers. Cook about 5 minutes, stirring often, until vegetables are tender. Whisk eggs in a large bowl and stir in cheese. Pour over sausage mixture and stir gently to distribute eggs evenly. Cook 2 to 3 minutes until set on the bottom and sides (eggs will still be runny in the center). Broil frittata 4 to 6 inches from heat source for about 3 minutes. Center will be firm. Serves 4.

Resa Creo, Savannah, GA

MYSTERY BARBECUE SANDWICHES

Drain a 5-ounce can of water-packed tuna. Combine with ¼ cup of your favorite barbecue sauce with onion bits. Heat and serve on heated buns. Everyone will think it's the best pork ever!

Anne S. Hanson, Albany, GA

Not everyone will love!

FRIED CHICKEN

My Grandmother Paul always said to season chicken and return it to the refrigerator and let it set as long as time permits, at least 2 to 3 hours. We season ours with House Seasoning and Lawry's Seasoned Salt.

3	eggs	1	1- to 2½-pound chicken, cut into pieces
⅓	cup water		Crisco shortening
2	cups self-rising flour		for frying
1	teaspoon pepper		

Beat eggs with water. To just enough self-rising flour to coat all the chicken, add black pepper. Dip seasoned chicken in egg; coat well in flour mixture. Fry in moderately hot shortening (350 degrees) until brown and crisp. Remember that dark meat requires longer cooking time (about 13 to 14 minutes, compared to 8 to 10 minutes for white meat). *the lady*

GARLIC CHICKEN

The men love this.

Toast 14 slices bread in slow oven until dry; make crumbs. Mix crumbs with ½ can Parmesan cheese and 3 teaspoons garlic salt. Melt 1½ sticks butter. Dip slightly salted chicken into melted butter, then roll in crumb mixture. Bake in an open Pyrex dish at 350 degrees for 1 hour.

Virginia Robertson, Albany, GA

NANCY'S SHRIMP AND NOODLES

1   8-ounce package egg noodles, or combination of spinach and egg noodles
2   pounds raw shrimp, peeled
1   stick butter
1 to 3 cloves garlic, chopped
¾   cup mayonnaise
1   can cream of mushroom soup
2   tablespoons chopped green onion

2   tablespoons chopped green pepper
¼   cup white wine
1   cup grated sharp Cheddar cheese
    Salt and pepper to taste
    Italian seasoning (optional)
1¼ cups sour cream

Cook noodles; drain and set aside. Sauté shrimp in butter and garlic until pink; set aside. Combine mayonnaise, mushroom soup, green onion, green pepper, and wine. Layer in a buttered casserole dish the noodles and soup mixture; pour shrimp over top. Bake at 350 degrees for 25 to 30 minutes. Top with sharp Cheddar cheese and bake another 5 minutes. Top with dollop of sour cream. This recipe is sinfully delicious. Serves 6.

Nancy Blood, Savannah, GA

CHICKEN NOODLE AND ASPARAGUS CASSEROLE

1   whole chicken
1   8-ounce package egg noodles
1   can cream of mushroom soup
1   can cream of chicken soup
1   cup mayonnaise

1   jar sliced mushrooms
1   jar pimentos
2   cans asparagus
1½ cups sharp Cheddar cheese
    Ritz crackers

Boil chicken (your way—I put in bell peppers, celery, onion, and seasonings). Save the chicken stock. Take chicken off bone when cooked; set aside. Boil egg noodles in the leftover stock and drain; set aside. Mix together soups, mayonnaise, mushrooms, and pimentos. In a casserole dish, layer egg noodles, chicken, asparagus, soup mixture, and ½ of the Cheddar cheese. Combine remaining cheese with Ritz crackers and sprinkle over top. Bake at 350 degrees for 45 minutes. This makes 2 small casseroles or 1 large. Variations: You can substitute broccoli for asparagus, and cashews can be substituted for Ritz crackers.

Nancy Blood, Savannah, GA

HONEY GAME HENS

6	Cornish game hens (about ¾ to 1 pound each)	½	cup soy sauce
4	cloves garlic, chopped	½	cup honey
1	1-inch piece of ginger, peeled and chopped	2	tablespoons peanut oil
		2	tablespoons orange juice
		1	tablespoon orange zest, minced

Rinse hens, trim off excess fat, and pat dry; place in bowl. Put garlic and ginger in food processor and process until nearly smooth. In another bowl, combine soy sauce, honey, oil, orange juice, and zest. Add the garlic and ginger. Pour mixture over game hens, coating well. Refrigerate overnight, turning in marinade several times. Preheat oven to 350 degrees. Place game hens in shallow roasting pan; pour marinade on top. Bake for 1 hour, basting every 15 minutes. Remove hens to serving platter. Pour cooking juices into small, heavy saucepan and boil for 5 minutes, or until sauce thickens. Pour over hens just before serving. Serve with sesame noodles or rice pilaf. These hens can also be grilled—just remember to baste often.

Nancy Blood, Savannah, GA

BARBECUE SHRIMP

3	pounds fresh shrimp, unpeeled	4	tablespoons freshly ground black pepper
1	stick butter		
2 to 3	tablespoons chopped garlic		

Preheat oven to 450 degrees. Wash and drain shrimp. Place in a shallow baking pan. Melt butter in a saucepan. Add garlic and sauté 3 to 4 minutes. Pour over shrimp and toss to coat. Pepper shrimp until shrimp are covered well. Bake until pink (about 5 minutes), turn, bake a few minutes longer, and pepper again. This will not be good unless you use a heavy hand with the pepper. Serve with a fresh garden salad and hot French bread. Dip bread in the pan juices for an extra treat. *Aunt Trina Bearden, Houma, LA*

SHRIMP GUMBO CASSEROLE

Diane is the mother of Misty, who is a server in our restaurant. Misty is a welcomed part of our staff. Thanks, Diane, for the contribution of your recipes and for having such a wonderful daughter.

1	cup finely chopped onion	1	10-ounce package frozen cut okra
1	cup finely chopped celery	1	teaspoon lemon-pepper seasoning
2	tablespoons olive oil	1½	teaspoons House Seasoning
1	14½-ounce can diced tomatoes	1	cup chicken or fish stock
2	bay leaves	2	cups shrimp, cleaned, peeled,
½	teaspoon dried thyme		and deveined

In an iron skillet, sauté onion and celery in oil. Add tomatoes, bay leaves, thyme, okra, lemon-pepper seasoning, and House Seasoning. Pour in stock. Cover pot and gently simmer for 30 minutes. Remove from heat and stir in shrimp. Prepare topping.

Topping

1	egg, beaten	1	12-ounce package
½	cup milk		corn muffin mix

Preheat oven to 400 degrees. Mix together egg and milk. In separate bowl, place muffin mix and add egg-milk mixture. Mix until just well blended. Drop by tablespoonfuls on top of hot shrimp mixture, leaving the center uncovered. Bake 15 to 20 minutes.   *Diane Silver Berryhill, Savannah, GA*

SAUSAGE RICE CASSEROLE

1	6-ounce box Uncle Ben's long-grain and wild rice	1	4-ounce can mushroom pieces
1	pound ground sausage	1	10¾-ounce can condensed cream of mushroom soup
2	small onions, chopped	½	stick butter

Preheat oven to 350 degrees. Cook rice according to directions on box. In a heavy skillet over medium heat, cook sausage until thoroughly done, about 4 to 5 minutes; drain. Combine all ingredients except butter and pour into casserole dish. Dot top with butter. Bake until bubbly, about 25 minutes.

the lady

PORK CHOPS IN TOMATO BARBECUE SAUCE

6   center-cut pork chops, trimmed
    of fat
1   tablespoon vegetable oil
1   14½-ounce can whole tomatoes,
    crushed
½   cup ketchup

¼   cup dark brown sugar
2   tablespoons Worcestershire
    sauce
2   tablespoons prepared mustard
½   teaspoon salt

Preheat oven to 350 degrees. Brown pork chops in oil. Drain, then place in a 13×9-inch baking dish. Combine remaining ingredients and spoon over chops. Bake for 45 minutes. Great served with macaroni and cheese!

Diane Silver Berryhill, Savannah, GA

CHICKEN BREASTS IN SOUR CREAM
WITH MUSHROOMS

8   slices dried beef (in a jar)
8   skinless boneless chicken
    breast halves (7 ounces each)
4   slices bacon, cut in half

1   cup sour cream
1   10¾-ounce can condensed
    cream of mushroom soup
2   cups sliced fresh mushrooms

Preheat oven to 300 degrees. Lay one piece of dried beef on each chicken breast and wrap with a half slice of bacon. Place in a 13×9-inch casserole dish, seam side down. Mix sour cream, soup, and mushrooms together. Pour over chicken breasts. Cover and bake for 1½ hours. Serve with rice. Serves 6 to 8.

Jill Hiers, Albany, GA

SUSAN'S SHRIMP AND MUSHROOM CASSEROLE

1   stick butter
¾   cup all-purpose flour
1½ cups half-and-half
1   10¾-ounce can condensed
     cream of mushroom soup
1   13¼-ounce can sliced
     mushrooms, drained

½   cup grated Parmesan cheese
1   pound cooked shrimp, peeled,
     deveined, and coarsely diced
     Garlic powder
     Buttered bread crumbs for
     topping

Preheat oven to 350 degrees. In saucepan over medium heat, melt butter
and stir in flour, then slowly blend in half-and-half, stirring constantly.
Sauce will be thick. Do not brown. Add mushroom soup, sliced
mushrooms, and Parmesan cheese. Fold in shrimp. Add garlic powder
to taste. Pour mixture into buttered casserole dish and top with buttered
bread crumbs. Bake for 25 to 30 minutes.

the lady

POT ROAST

*Put this on to cook in the slow cooker before leaving for work
and come home in the evening to a mouthwatering dinner.*

1   3-pound boneless chuck roast
1½ teaspoons House Seasoning
¼   cup vegetable oil
1   onion, thinly sliced
3   bay leaves

3 or 4 beef bouillon cubes, crushed
2   cloves garlic, crushed
1   10¾-ounce can condensed
     cream of mushroom soup
¼ to ½ cup Chardonnay wine

Sprinkle roast on all sides with House Seasoning; season well. In
moderately hot skillet, brown roast on all sides in oil. Place roast in Crock-
Pot. On top of the roast, layer onion, bay leaves, crushed beef bouillon
cubes, crushed garlic, and cream of mushroom soup. Add Chardonnay.
Cover with just enough water to cover all the ingredients sufficiently.
Cook on low setting approximately 8 hours.

the lady

MEAT LOAF

1	pound ground beef	1	egg, lightly beaten
1¼	teaspoons salt	8	ounces canned diced tomatoes,
¼	teaspoon ground black pepper		with juice
½	cup chopped onion	½	cup quick-cooking oats
½	cup chopped bell pepper		

Preheat oven to 375 degrees. Mix all meat loaf ingredients well and place in a baking dish. Shape into a loaf. Mix ⅓ cup ketchup, 2 tablespoons brown sugar, and 1 tablespoon prepared mustard. Spread on loaf. Bake for 1 hour. Serves 4.   *Peggy Ort, Albany, GA*

SHRIMP TEMPURA

1	cup all-purpose flour	2	tablespoons melted fat or
½	teaspoon sugar		vegetable oil
½	teaspoon salt	2	pounds uncooked shrimp,
1	cup ice water		peeled and deveined,
1	egg		tails left on
			Vegetable oil for deep-frying

In a large bowl, stir together flour, sugar, and salt. Beat in ice water, egg, and 2 tablespoons fat or oil. Dry shrimp thoroughly. In a large, heavy pot, heat oil for deep-frying until it registers 375 degrees. Holding shrimp by tails, dip in batter. Carefully place in pot and fry until golden brown. Do not overcook; just a few minutes does the trick. Drain on paper towels and serve immediately. Serves 4 to 6.   *the lady*

FRUIT PIZZA (KIDS LOVE IT)

1   16½-ounce package refrigerated
   sugar cookie dough
1   8-ounce package cream cheese,
   softened
⅓   cup granulated sugar
1   teaspoon vanilla extract

2   cups fresh fruit
   (make it colorful: use
   strawberries, kiwis,
   blueberries, peaches, etc.)
1   10-ounce jar peach
   or apricot jelly

Lightly grease round pizza pan. Cut cookie dough into ⅛-inch slices, sealing dough edges to make crust. Leave a little space at the edge of your pan, unless the pan has sides, because the dough expands when baked. Bake until light brown, 10 to 12 minutes; let cool. In a bowl, combine cream cheese, sugar, and vanilla; mix well. Spread over cooked crust. Arrange fruit in a decorative pattern on top of cream cheese mixture. Heat jelly until runny. Spoon over fruit to glaze. Refrigerate until ready to serve. *Variations:* You can substitute a liqueur for the jelly. Also, you can basically make this type of recipe using 2 rolls of Pillsbury crescent rolls and cream cheese, topped with fresh veggies: broccoli florets, olives, shredded carrots, etc.   *Nancy Blood, Savannah, GA*

"When you eat at The Lady & Sons, it's like being home
at the dinner table. Thanks for a good home-cooked meal."

"No one in this town does it better."

Vegetables

Did you ever have one of those days when you had to stop & ask yourself, Did I have the kids with me when I left the house today?

ASPARAGUS CASSEROLE

Aunt Jessie is my dad's older sister and she is very dear and special.
I have always known that she was just a phone call away. She and
my daddy had a wonderful relationship, and she was much loved
by my daddy and mother.

2 tablespoons butter	1 cup grated Cheddar cheese
2 tablespoons all-purpose flour	4 hard-boiled eggs, sliced
2 cups milk	Salt and pepper to taste
2 15-ounce cans asparagus spears, drained	1 cup breadcrumbs

To make sauce, heat butter in a skillet; stir in flour, mixing well, then
add milk all at once. Cook over medium heat, stirring constantly, until
thick and creamy; set aside. Arrange half of the asparagus in bottom of a
buttered 2-quart casserole. Top with half of the Cheddar cheese and half of
the egg slices. Sprinkle with salt and pepper. Pour half of the sauce on top.
Repeat layers, beginning with remaining asparagus. Top with breadcrumbs
and bake at 350 degrees for 30 minutes. Serves 6.

Jessie R. Dixon, Eagle Lake, FL

SUSAN'S BAKED RICE

1 large onion, chopped	1 cup uncooked white rice
1 large bell pepper, chopped	2 cups water
1 stick butter	Ground black pepper
4 or 5 chicken bouillon cubes	to taste

Preheat oven to 350 degrees. Sauté onion and bell pepper in butter; add
bouillon cubes. Stir until dissolved. Combine rice and water and add to
mixture. Pour into a 13×9-inch baking dish. Sprinkle with pepper. Bake
for 45 minutes. Goes great with baked or fried chicken.

the lady

SAVORY BROWN RICE

1	cup uncooked rice	1	teaspoon butter
1	medium onion	2	bouillon cubes, beef or
1	bell pepper		chicken
1	#2 can sliced mushrooms	2	cups boiling water

Brown rice, onion, pepper, and mushrooms in butter. Add bouillon cubes to boiling water and stir into brown rice mixture. Transfer to casserole dish and bake at 350 degrees for about 1 hour.   *Jacklyn Miller, Guyton, GA*

SQUASH CASSEROLE

3	cups cooked squash, drained	1	large onion, chopped
1	can cream of chicken soup	1	stick butter
1	8-ounce carton sour cream	1	package Pepperidge Farm
1	small jar pimentos		dressing

Combine all ingredients and pour into casserole dish. Bake at 350 degrees for 45 minutes.   *Jacklyn Miller, Guyton, GA*

ZUCCHINI-CORN CASSEROLE

1½	pounds small zucchini	1	tablespoon butter
1	8-ounce can cream-style corn	½	teaspoon salt
2	eggs, lightly beaten	¼	teaspoon ground black pepper
1	small onion, chopped	½	cup grated sharp Cheddar cheese
1	small bell pepper, chopped		Paprika to taste

Preheat oven to 350 degrees. Cook zucchini in boiling salted water to cover until just tender, about 6 minutes. Drain, cut into chunks, and combine with corn and eggs. Meanwhile, sauté onion and bell pepper in butter until golden brown, about 5 minutes. Add to zucchini and corn mixture; add salt and pepper. Pour mixture into a greased casserole. Sprinkle cheese on top, then sprinkle with paprika. Bake uncovered for about 30 minutes, or until lightly browned and bubbly. Makes 4 to 5 servings.   *Janet DiClaudio, Savannah, GA*

ZUCCHINI CUSTARD CASSEROLE

½   stick butter, melted
2   pounds zucchini, cut into small
    pieces
3   eggs
½   cup undiluted evaporated milk or
    light cream
2   tablespoons fine dry bread crumbs

1   teaspoon instant minced onion
1   teaspoon Worcestershire sauce
    Dash of liquid hot pepper
    sauce
¾   teaspoon salt
⅛   teaspoon pepper
⅓   cup grated Parmesan cheese

Preheat oven to 350 degrees. In a large saucepan with a tight-fitting lid, combine melted butter and zucchini. Cover and cook over low heat, stirring occasionally, until tender (5 to 7 minutes). Remove from heat and set aside. Beat eggs with milk; add bread crumbs, onion, Worcestershire sauce, hot pepper sauce, salt, pepper, and 2 tablespoons of the Parmesan. Mix well. Combine mixture with zucchini, stirring until blended. Turn into a buttered 1½-quart casserole. Sprinkle top with remaining Parmesan cheese. Bake uncovered for 35 to 40 minutes. If the dish has been refrigerated, allow about 10 minutes longer baking time. Serves 4 to 6.

Janet DiClaudio, Savannah, GA

VIDALIA ONION CASSEROLE

4   large Vidalia onions, quartered
7   tablespoons butter
3   eggs
1   5-ounce can evaporated milk

1   tube Ritz Crackers,
    crushed
1½ cups grated Cheddar cheese
    Salt and pepper to taste

In a saucepan, boil onions until tender; drain. In a skillet, heat 4 tablespoons of the butter, and sauté onions. In a large bowl, beat eggs and milk together. Add onions, half of the cracker crumbs, the Cheddar cheese, salt, and pepper. Pour into a buttered casserole, and bake at 375 degrees for 35 minutes. Melt remaining 3 tablespoons butter and stir into remaining cracker crumbs. Top casserole with buttered crumbs and bake for 15 minutes longer.

Sheila Mims, Albany, GA

ONION CASSEROLE

6	tablespoons butter	1	cup cracker crumbs
3	medium onions, peeled and sliced	2	eggs
¼	cup chopped green pepper	¾	cup milk
2	tablespoons chopped pimento	1	teaspoon salt
1	cup grated sharp cheese	⅛	teaspoon white pepper

Melt 4 tablespoons of the butter in skillet; add onions and green pepper. Sauté until tender; stir in pimento. Place half of the onion mixture in baking dish; sprinkle with half of the cheese and ¼ cup of the cracker crumbs. Layer on remaining halves of onion mixture and cheese. Beat eggs with milk; add salt and white pepper; pour over onions and cheese. Cook until mixture is set, approximately 30 to 35 minutes at 350 degrees. Melt remaining butter. Cover casserole with remaining crumbs and drizzle with melted butter. Bake an additional 15 minutes.

Jean Gregory, Brunswick, GA

GREEN PEPPER CASSEROLE

1	cup uncooked rice	1	cup chopped celery
2	tablespoons butter, melted	1	garlic clove, minced
3	green peppers, cut into strips	1	15-ounce can tomato sauce
3	chicken bouillon cubes	1	teaspoon oregano
2	cups boiling water	1	teaspoon salt
1	pound ground beef	¼	teaspoon black pepper
1	cup chopped onion	1½	cups shredded Cheddar cheese

Cook rice in melted butter in skillet until lightly toasted, stirring frequently. Spread in greased 13×9-inch baking dish. Arrange green pepper strips on top of rice. Dissolve bouillon cubes in boiling water and pour over rice mixture. Cover with foil. Bake at 375 degrees for 20 minutes. In the meantime, cook ground beef, onion, celery, and garlic in skillet until meat is browned. Stir in tomato sauce, oregano, salt, and black pepper. Simmer, covered, for 5 minutes. Pour over peppers and rice. Cover and continue baking for 15 more minutes. Remove from oven; sprinkle with cheese and bake for approximately 5 more minutes, uncovered.

Denise Watson, Albany, GA

CABBAGE CASSEROLE

1 large head cabbage	Dash of pepper
2 eggs	1 tablespoon butter
1 cup sour cream	¼ cup grated Cheddar
1 teaspoon salt	cheese

Preheat oven to 350 degrees. Remove outer leaves from cabbage; shred and cover with boiling water. Boil for 5 minutes; drain. Beat eggs until foamy; add sour cream, salt, and pepper; beat until smooth. Stir in cabbage and pour into greased 2-quart casserole. Dot with butter; sprinkle with grated cheese. Bake for 30 minutes. Serves 4 to 6.

Denise Watson, Albany, GA

CABBAGE CASSEROLE

1 medium cabbage, shredded	1 cup shredded cheese
1 green pepper, chopped	1 can cream of chicken soup
1 onion, chopped	Salt to taste
8 slices bacon, diced and cooked	

Boil cabbage and drain; add pepper and onion. Mix remaining ingredients and combine with cabbage. Put in casserole dish and bake at 350 degrees for 45 minutes. *Variation:* 2 cups medium white sauce can be substituted for cream of chicken soup.

Jill Hiers, Albany, GA

SWEET POTATO CHIPS

Helen is one of my Aunt Peggy's cooking buddies.
Boy, do they have a good time when they get together.

2 large sweet potatoes	1 cup honey-roasted peanuts, chopped
1 stick butter, melted	Salt to taste

Preheat oven to 450 degrees. Line two large baking sheets with foil; lightly grease. Slice potatoes to ¼ inch thick. Dip potatoes in melted butter and arrange on baking sheet so that chips do not overlap. Sprinkle with peanuts. Bake for 15 to 20 minutes. Sprinkle with salt.

Helen Rooks, Albany, GA

PINEAPPLE CASSEROLE

1	cup sugar	2	20-ounce cans pineapple chunks,
6	tablespoons all-purpose flour		drained (reserve 6 tablespoons juice)
2	cups grated sharp Cheddar	1	cup Ritz cracker crumbs
	cheese	1	stick butter, melted

Preheat oven to 350 degrees. In a mixing bowl, combine sugar and flour. Gradually stir in cheese. Add pineapple and stir well. Pour mixture into a greased casserole dish. Combine cracker crumbs, butter, and pineapple juice and spread on top of pineapple mixture. Bake for 25 to 30 minutes or until golden brown.

CHEESY BROCCOLI BAKE

2	pounds fresh broccoli, trimmed and cut up	1	10¾-ounce can condensed cream of mushroom soup
¼	cup chopped celery	½	pound Velveeta
¼	pound fresh mushrooms, sliced	½	teaspoon garlic salt
¼	cup chopped onion	¼	teaspoon pepper
2	tablespoons butter	1	cup grated Cheddar
1	8-ounce can sliced water chestnuts		cheese

Preheat oven to 350 degrees. Steam broccoli for 10 minutes. Sauté celery, mushrooms, and onion in butter for 10 minutes; drain. Combine broccoli, sauté mixture, and water chestnuts. Heat soup and Velveeta in saucepan over low heat until cheese melts. Pour over broccoli mixture. Stir in garlic salt and pepper. Place in greased casserole dish. Bake for 25 minutes. Sprinkle top with grated Cheddar. Serves 8 to 10.   *Jill Hiers, Albany, GA*

VEGETABLE CASSEROLE

1 15-ounce can Veg-All, drained
1 8-ounce can sliced water
   chestnuts, drained
1 cup grated sharp cheese
1 cup chopped celery

¾ cup mayonnaise
1 small onion, chopped
20 Ritz Crackers, crushed
2 tablespoons butter, melted

In a large bowl, mix Veg-All, water chestnuts, cheese, celery, mayonnaise, and onion; transfer to a greased casserole. Bake at 350 degrees for 30 minutes. Combine cracker crumbs and butter. When casserole has baked for 30 minutes, sprinkle with buttered crumbs and return to oven to brown.

the lady

CREAMED CORN

1 dozen ears fresh corn
1 stick butter

Salt and pepper to taste

Remove corn from cob using a corn grater. (If you have to cut corn with a knife, avoid whole kernels; try mashing a little.) Put corn in glass dish and put stick of butter on top. Cook in microwave on high about 7 to 10 minutes, stopping to turn and stir a couple of times. Be careful not to overcook corn. If it seems too dry, add a little milk or water. Season with salt and pepper to taste.

the lady

CREAMED POTATOES

8 to 10 medium red potatoes,
   skin on
½ cup hot milk

½ cup butter
½ cup sour cream
Salt and black pepper to taste

Cook potatoes either whole or sliced. We cook our red potatoes whole because we never know for what use we will need them. Cook with the skins on for the nutrient value. Whip unpeeled, cooked potatoes with electric mixer until moderately smooth. Don't overbeat them; a few lumps are nice. Add hot milk, butter, sour cream, and salt and black pepper. Whip until creamy. Adjust thickness by adding more milk, if desired.

the lady

TURNIP GREENS WITH CORNMEAL DUMPLINGS

¾	pound smoked meat (smoked turkey wings are excellent)	¼	teaspoon ground ginger
4	quarts water	1	bunch turnip greens with roots
1	teaspoon House Seasoning	½	stick butter
2	chicken bouillon cubes	1	teaspoon sugar (optional; may be used if greens are bitter)

Place smoked meat in water along with House Seasoning, bouillon, and ginger. Cook over low heat for 1½ hours. Strip turnip leaves free of the big stem that runs down the center of each leaf. Wash in a sink full of clean water. Drain and wash twice more, since greens can often be sandy. Peel and slice or quarter roots. Add greens to meat; cook for another 30 minutes, stirring often. Add roots and continue to cook for approximately 15 minutes or until roots are tender. (Reserve ⅔ cup liquid after cooking if making dumplings.) Add butter and dumplings (if desired) and serve.

Cornmeal Dumplings

1	cup all-purpose cornmeal	1	egg
½	teaspoon salt	⅔	cup liquid from cooked turnips
1	small onion, chopped		

Mix all ingredients together. Dipping by teaspoonfuls, gently roll batter in the palms of your hands into approximately 1-inch balls; drop into boiling turnip liquid. Make sure each dumpling is completely covered in liquid by shaking the pot gently; do not stir. Boil for about 10 minutes.

COLLARD GREENS

One day while eating in the restaurant, "Mr. B." Williams whispered into my ear, "Paula, try putting a little ginger in your greens next time, I think you will like it." He was right, and when I'm in charge of cooking the collards, to this day, I always add ginger.

Collard greens are cooked much the same way as turnip greens, but collards will not shrink as much. Strip the leaves from the stems, roll and chop leaves, and proceed as with turnips. *Hint:* If you don't want cooked collards to smell up the house, wash one whole pecan unshelled and add it to the pot.

the Lady

SWEET POTATO CASSEROLE

4	large unpeeled sweet potatoes (enough to yield 3 cups mashed)	1	teaspoon ground nutmeg
1	cup sugar	1	cup sour cream
1	stick butter, melted		Pinch of salt
3	eggs, beaten		Pinch of baking soda
1	teaspoon vanilla extract		Miniature marshmallows, pecans, or raisins, for topping (optional)

Boil sweet potatoes. Peel and place in a mixing bowl. Mash well. Add sugar, butter, eggs, vanilla, nutmeg, and sour cream; mix well. Stir in salt and baking soda. Spread mixture in 1½-quart casserole dish and bake uncovered at 350 degrees for 35 to 45 minutes. When done, place marshmallows on top and return casserole to oven until marshmallows are melted and lightly browned.   *Violet Summerall, Hinesville, GA*

BROCCOLI SOUFFLÉ

3	10-ounce packages frozen chopped broccoli	2	teaspoons chopped fresh parsley
¾	cup chicken stock	3	tablespoons minced onion
¾	cup whipping cream		Salt and pepper to taste
1	stick butter	½	cup grated Monterey Jack or Cheddar cheese
½	cup all-purpose flour		
4	eggs, separated		

Preheat oven to 425 degrees. Cook and drain broccoli. Add stock to cream and scald. Melt butter and blend in flour. Gradually add to cream mixture. Stir over medium heat until thick. Remove from heat and beat in egg yolks, parsley, onion, salt, and pepper. Stir in broccoli and cheese. When ready to serve, add stiffly beaten egg whites and pour into a buttered casserole dish. Bake for 25 to 30 minutes. Serves 10.   *the lady*

SQUASH AND CHEESE CASSEROLE

1 cup milk
3 tablespoons butter
1 cup bread crumbs
2 cups cooked, mashed squash
1 cup grated Cheddar cheese

1 tablespoon grated onion
Salt and pepper to taste
2 eggs, well beaten
Buttered bread crumbs,
for topping (optional)

In a small saucepan, heat milk and butter until butter melts; pour over crumbs; mix well. Stir in squash, cheese, onion, and seasonings, then add eggs. Pour into casserole dish and bake at 350 degrees for 25 to 30 minutes. *Variation:* Sprinkle buttered bread crumbs on top before baking.

TOMATO PIE

Mildred, along with her mother, and Dot Smith have been frequent guests in our restaurant. It's always a pleasure to see them walking through the door. Thanks, ladies.

4 tomatoes, peeled and sliced
8 to 10 fresh basil leaves, chopped
⅓ cup chopped green onion
1 9-inch prebaked deep-dish pie shell

Salt and pepper to taste
2 cups grated mozzarella and Cheddar cheese (combined)
1 cup mayonnaise

Preheat oven to 350 degrees. Layer tomato slices, basil, and onion in pie shell. Add salt and pepper to taste. Mix together grated cheese and mayonnaise. Spread on top of tomatoes. Bake for 30 minutes or until lightly browned. *Mrs. Henry Ambos, Savannah, GA*

HOPPIN' JOHNS

2 cups black-eyed peas, cooked
2 cups cooked rice
1 small onion, chopped

1 small bell pepper, chopped
Garlic powder to taste

Heat the black-eyed peas and add the rice. Add remaining ingredients and cook an additional 10 to 15 minutes. Do not overcook. This dish is best if the bell pepper and onion still have a crunch to them.

BROWN RICE

1	cup chopped onion	1	small can sliced mushrooms,
1	stick butter		drained
1	can beef consommé	1	cup uncooked rice
1	can onion soup		

In saucepan over medium heat, sauté onion in butter until almost tender. Remove from heat. Stir in consommé, onion soup, mushrooms, and uncooked rice. Pour into casserole dish. Bake at 350 degrees for about 1 hour, or until done.

the lady

EGGPLANT CASSEROLE

1	large eggplant	2	eggs
1¾	cups crushed Ritz crackers	⅔	cup milk
1½	cups grated American cheese	1	teaspoon House Seasoning
1	stick butter, melted		

Preheat oven to 350 degrees. Peel, slice, and boil eggplant for 10 to 15 minutes, until tender; drain. Divide cracker crumbs, cheese, and butter in half. To eggplant, add eggs, milk, House Seasoning, and half the crumbs, cheese, and butter. Mix well; pour into baking dish. Top with remaining half of the crumbs, cheese, and butter. Bake for 20 to 30 minutes.

the lady

BROCCOLI CASSEROLE

1	package frozen chopped broccoli	1	8-ounce jar Cheez Whiz
1	can cream of chicken soup	1	can water chestnuts, chopped
1	cup cooked rice		Buttered bread cubes

Prepare broccoli as directed on package; drain. Add chicken soup, rice, Cheez Whiz, and water chestnuts; pour into baking dish. Top with buttered bread cubes, and bake at 325 degrees for 35 to 40 minutes. Serves 2 to 3.

the lady

FRIED GREEN TOMATOES

Quite frequently I walk the dining room with a plate piled high of this wonderful fried fruit. The guests seem to enjoy this extra treat. My grandmother always used cornmeal, but I prefer flour. So this is optional.

3 or 4 large, firm green tomatoes
    Salt
2   cups self-rising flour or cornmeal

1 to 2 teaspoons pepper
Vegetable oil for frying

Slice tomatoes to desired thickness (I prefer mine thin). Lay out on a pan and sprinkle with salt. Place in a colander and allow time for salt to pull the water out of tomatoes. Mix flour with pepper. Coat tomatoes with flour mixture and deep-fry until golden brown.

the lady

BROCCOLI CASSEROLE

1   10-ounce package frozen chopped broccoli
1   small onion, chopped
½   stick butter
½   cup grated Cheddar cheese

½   cup crushed Ritz crackers
½   cup condensed cream of mushroom soup
¼   cup mayonnaise
    House Seasoning to taste

Preheat oven to 350 degrees. Steam broccoli until limp, about 10 minutes. Remove from heat; drain. Sauté onion in butter and add to broccoli. Add all remaining ingredients; mix well. Pour mixture into a casserole dish. Add topping. Serves 2 to 3.

Topping

½   cup crushed Ritz crackers

1   tablespoon butter, melted

Combine crackers and melted butter for topping; sprinkle on top of casserole. Bake for 20 to 25 minutes.

the lady

SHERRY-GLAZED SWEET POTATOES

3	large sweet potatoes or yams	½ cup brown sugar
6	slices canned pineapple	½ cup sherry
½	stick butter	

Preheat oven to 375 degrees. Boil potatoes, with skins on, for 20 to
30 minutes, or until tender. Drain and allow to cool. Peel and cut
lengthwise into halves. Arrange slices of pineapple in a single layer in
a greased shallow baking dish; place a potato half (cut side down) on top
of each pineapple slice. Heat butter, brown sugar, and sherry together until
sugar is dissolved; pour over potatoes and pineapple. Bake for
30 minutes, basting often with syrup in dish. Serves 6.   *the lady*

CORN CASSEROLE

1	15¼-ounce can whole-kernel corn, drained	1 8-ounce package Jiffy Corn Muffin Mix
1	14¾-ounce can cream-style corn	1 cup sour cream
		1 stick butter, melted

In a large bowl, stir together two cans corn, corn muffin mix, sour cream,
and butter. Pour into a greased casserole. Bake at 350 degrees for 45 to 60
minutes, or until golden brown.   *Aileen Patton, Carson, CA*

SWEET POTATO BALLS

4 large sweet potatoes	2 cups shredded coconut
⅔ cup packed brown sugar	½ cup granulated sugar
2 tablespoons orange juice	1 teaspoon ground cinnamon
1 teaspoon orange zest	8 large marshmallows
½ teaspoon freshly grated nutmeg	

Bake potatoes until tender, then peel and mash (potatoes can be baked the day before). In a medium bowl, combine mashed potatoes, brown sugar, orange juice, zest, and nutmeg. In a shallow dish, toss coconut with granulated sugar and cinnamon. Press mashed potatoes around each marshmallow, then roll balls in coconut mixture. Bake at 350 degrees for 15 to 20 minutes. Watch carefully during last few minutes of cooking; expanding marshmallows can cause potato balls to burst open. These are wonderful served with turkey or ham.   *Shelly Peay, Richmond Hill, GA*

SWEET POTATO CASSEROLE

3 cups peeled, cooked, and mashed sweet potatoes or yams	1 teaspoon vanilla extract
	1 teaspoon ground cinnamon
1 cup sugar	¼ teaspoon ground nutmeg
⅓ cup butter, melted	¼ cup heavy cream, half-and-half,
2 eggs	or whole milk

Preheat oven to 325 degrees. Mix all ingredients together except for cream. Beat with electric mixer until smooth. Add cream; mix well. Pour into greased casserole dish. Add topping. Bake for 25 to 30 minutes.

Topping

1 cup brown sugar	⅓ cup all-purpose flour
1 cup walnuts, chopped	3 tablespoons butter, melted

Mix together with fork; sprinkle over top of casserole.   *the lady*

81

FRESH CORN SCALLOP

6	ears fresh corn	⅛	teaspoon pepper
2	tablespoons all-purpose flour	½	cup milk
1	teaspoon sugar	¾	cup buttered dry
1¼	teaspoons salt		bread crumbs

Preheat oven to 375 degrees. Cut corn off cob, being careful not to cut too deep. This should make 2½ to 3 cups of corn. Combine corn, flour, sugar, salt, pepper, and milk. Sprinkle half the crumbs over bottom of 1-quart casserole dish. Add corn mixture. Bake covered for 30 minutes. Remove cover and sprinkle with remaining crumbs. Bake uncovered 20 minutes more. Makes 6 servings.   *Diane Silver Berryhill, Savannah, GA*

POTATO CASSEROLE
Leftover mashed potatoes work wonderfully in this recipe.

2	cups mashed potatoes	1	stick butter
½	cup sour cream	1½	cups grated Cheddar
	House Seasoning to taste		cheese
1	small onion, sliced thin	4	medium potatoes, cooked
1	small bell pepper, sliced thin	6	slices bacon, cooked crisp

Preheat oven to 350 degrees. Spread mashed potatoes evenly on bottom of casserole dish. Layer sour cream evenly over top. (Each time you add a layer, sprinkle on a little House Seasoning.) Sauté onion and bell pepper in butter; evenly layer over top of sour cream. Next, layer with ½ cup Cheddar cheese. Slice potatoes and layer over cheese until top is completely covered with potatoes. Finally, top with remaining 1 cup cheese. Bake for 25 to 30 minutes. Remove from oven and crumble bacon over top.   *the Lady*

BAKED GRITS

4 cups water	1½ cups grated Monterey Jack
1½ teaspoons salt	and Cheddar cheese
1 cup uncooked grits	(combined)
2 eggs, beaten	2 cloves garlic, crushed
1 stick butter	Dash of cayenne pepper

Preheat oven to 350 degrees. Bring water and salt to a boil. Add grits to boiling water, stirring constantly for a minute. Cover and cook, stirring occasionally, until grits are thick and creamy. Temper eggs with a small amount of hot cooked grits, then add back to remaining grits. Combine remaining ingredients with grits and pour into a 2-quart casserole dish. Bake for 45 minutes. Top with additional cheese, if desired.   *the lady*

HOT FRUIT

1 can pear halves	½ cup dark brown sugar
1 can chunky pineapple	½ tablespoon curry powder
1 can peach halves	½ teaspoon ground cinnamon
1 jar maraschino cherries	½ teaspoon ground nutmeg
⅓ cup cold butter	

Drain fruit and arrange all but maraschino cherries in shallow 2-quart baking dish. Place a cherry in center of each fruit half. Combine butter, sugar, and spices and crumble over fruit. Bake at 375 degrees for 30 to 40 minutes. This is better if baked a day in advance and reheated just before serving. Very good with baked ham.   *Nancy Snowden, Savannah, GA*

BECKY'S BEST BAKED BEANS

½ pound bacon	5 tablespoons maple or
1 large onion, diced	pancake syrup
1 16-ounce can pork and beans	4 tablespoons ketchup
3 tablespoons yellow mustard	

Preheat oven to 325 degrees. Fry bacon until crisp; crumble. In bacon drippings, sauté onion until brown. Mix bacon, onion, and drippings with remaining ingredients. Pour into casserole dish and bake covered for 45 to 60 minutes.   *Becky Cohen, Savannah, GA*

SQUASH CASSEROLE

1	large onion, chopped	1	cup crushed Ritz crackers, plus additional for topping
½	stick butter		
3	cups cooked squash, drained, with all water squeezed out	½	cup sour cream
		1	teaspoon House Seasoning
		1	cup grated Cheddar cheese

Preheat oven to 350 degrees. Sauté onion in butter for 5 minutes. Remove from pan and mix all ingredients together. Pour into buttered casserole dish and top with cracker crumbs. Bake for 25 to 30 minutes.   *the lady*

BOURSIN CHEESE POTATOES

3	pounds red potatoes, unpeeled	1	5-ounce package Boursin cheese
	Salt and pepper to taste		
1	pint heavy cream		Fresh chives or parsley, chopped

Preheat oven to 350 degrees. Wash and slice potatoes into ¼-inch-thick rounds. Toss potatoes with salt and pepper. Heat cream and cheese together, on top of stove or in microwave, until cheese has melted. Stir mixture until thoroughly blended. Layer half of the potatoes into a 2-quart baking dish (this is best if done in a deep dish instead of a long, flat dish). Cover potatoes with half of the cream mixture. Repeat with remaining potatoes and cream mixture. Cover and bake for 1 hour. Sprinkle top with chopped chives or parsley.   *Kelley Ort, Atlanta, GA*

PERFECT POTATO PUDDING

1 8-ounce carton sour cream
¾ cup milk
1 1¼-ounce package sour cream
   sauce mix
3 cups uncooked shredded hash
   brown potatoes

Salt and pepper to taste
Dill weed to taste
½ cup buttered bread crumbs
¼ cup Parmesan cheese
   (optional)

Heat (do not boil) sour cream. Combine milk and sour cream sauce mix, blend well with sour cream. In a buttered 1-quart casserole, layer potatoes, sour cream mixture, and seasonings alternately. Cover with bread crumbs and Parmesan cheese. Bake at 350 degrees for 30 minutes, or until brown and bubbly. Frozen shredded hash browns are great in this recipe. Defrost first and separate carefully.   *Anne S. Hanson, Albany, GA*

PEA PODS WITH GRAND MARNIER

1 cup water
1 teaspoon sugar
3 10-ounce packages frozen
   snow peas
1 8-ounce can sliced water
   chestnuts, drained

¼ cup Grand Marnier
5 tablespoons butter
1 tablespoon chopped fresh mint,
   or 1½ tablespoons dried mint
1 teaspoon salt

In a saucepan, bring water to a boil and add sugar. Drop in snow peas and cook until barely tender, drain, and return to pan. Add water chestnuts, Grand Marnier, butter, mint, and salt. Cook over medium-low heat until heated through.   *Anne S. Hanson, Albany, GA*

Breads

Straight to the horse's mouth...

Caution! When following one of Savannah's carriage tours, Be warned the horses brake for Paula's cheese biscuits!

CORNY CORNBREAD

1 cup self-rising cornmeal	2 eggs
¾ cup self-rising flour	1 cup sour cream
½ cup vegetable oil plus ¼ cup	1 cup grated sharp Cheddar cheese
for skillet	½ teaspoon cayenne pepper
1 8-ounce can cream-style corn	(optional)

Preheat oven to 375 degrees. Mix all ingredients together. Pour into a heated cast-iron skillet that has been well greased with oil. Bake until golden brown, approximately 30 minutes.

the lady

MONKEY BREAD

½ cup granulated sugar	½ cup chopped pecans
3 teaspoons ground cinnamon	1 stick butter
3 cans 10-count biscuits	1 cup brown sugar

Mix sugar and cinnamon. Cut biscuits into fourths; roll in sugar-cinnamon mixture. Sprinkle chopped pecans into a greased pan; place individual biscuit pieces over nuts. In a saucepan, melt butter and brown sugar over low heat. Pour over biscuit mixture. Bake in preheated oven at 350 degrees for 30 minutes.   *Resa Creo, Savannah, GA*

SOUR CREAM MUFFINS

2 cups self-rising flour	1 cup sour cream
2 sticks butter, at room temperature	

Preheat oven to 400 degrees. In a medium bowl, mix flour and butter together; add sour cream, and blend well. Place spoonfuls of batter in greased miniature muffin pans. Bake for 8 to 10 minutes, or until golden.

Susan Williams, Albany, GA

When Susan's grandchildren were born, they called her "Bubbles," and it stuck. Bubbles has been my best friend and by my side for over 30 years.

ZUCCHINI BREAD

The flavor improves with age and the bread keeps well frozen.
You can also substitute pumpkin for zucchini.

3¼ cups all-purpose flour
1½ teaspoons salt
1 teaspoon ground nutmeg
2 teaspoons baking soda
1 teaspoon ground cinnamon
3 cups sugar

1 cup vegetable oil
4 eggs, beaten
⅔ cup water
2 cups grated zucchini
1 teaspoon lemon juice
1 cup chopped walnuts or pecans

Preheat oven to 350 degrees. Mix dry ingredients except for nuts in a large bowl. In a separate bowl, mix wet ingredients; fold into dry, and add nuts. Bake in two loaf pans for 1 hour, or until done. *the lady*

CLEMENT'S BANANA NUT BREAD

½ cup Crisco shortening
1 cup sugar
2 cups all-purpose flour
1 teaspoon salt
2 teaspoons baking powder

½ teaspoon baking soda
2 eggs, beaten
3 bananas, mashed
⅓ cup buttermilk
½ cup chopped walnuts or pecans

Preheat oven to 350 degrees. Cream shortening and sugar. Sift together flour, salt, baking powder, and baking soda and add to creamed mixture. Add remaining ingredients; mix well. Pour into a well-greased loaf pan. Bake for 40 to 45 minutes. *the lady*

EASY ROLLS

1 cup self-rising flour
½ cup milk

1 teaspoon sugar
2 tablespoons mayonnaise

Preheat oven to 350 degrees. Mix together flour and milk. Add sugar and mayonnaise. Pour into slightly greased muffin tins and bake for 12 to 15 minutes. *the lady*

YEAST BISCUITS

1 package yeast	1 tablespoon baking powder
½ cup lukewarm water	2 tablespoons sugar
5 cups all-purpose flour	¾ cup Crisco shortening
1 teaspoon baking soda	2 cups buttermilk
1 teaspoon salt	

Preheat oven to 400 degrees. Dissolve yeast in warm water; set aside. Mix dry ingredients together. Cut in shortening. Add yeast and buttermilk and mix well. Turn dough onto lightly floured surface and roll out to desired thickness. Cut with small biscuit cutter and place on greased baking sheet. Bake for 12 minutes or until golden brown.

GRANDMOTHER PAUL'S FRITTERS

1¾ cups all-purpose flour	1 cup milk
1 tablespoon sugar	1 tablespoon shortening, melted
3 teaspoons baking powder	
1 teaspoon salt	2 cups chopped vegetables
½ teaspoon pepper	(cooked or canned), or
1 egg, lightly beaten	chopped fruit, well drained

Sift flour; measure. Add sugar, baking powder, salt, and pepper; sift again. Combine egg, milk, and melted shortening. Pour into flour mixture and stir until just smooth. Add chopped vegetables or fruit. Drop by tablespoonfuls into deep hot fat and fry 3 to 5 minutes, or until brown all over. *Secret:* If using fruit, add 1 tablespoon sugar to the flour mixture. If fruit is tart, increase sugar to 2 or 3 tablespoons.

DUTCH BREAD

1	package yeast	6	cups all-purpose flour
½	cup warm water	2	cups scalded milk
2	tablespoons sugar	2	tablespoons Crisco
1½	teaspoons salt		shortening

Preheat oven to 375 degrees. Mix yeast in water and set aside to dissolve. Combine dry ingredients. Add milk, shortening, and yeast. Pour into two greased 8×4×3-inch pans. Bake for approximately 45 to 50 minutes.

Alberta DiClaudio, Savannah, GA

PEANUT BUTTER BREAD

2	cups all-purpose flour	4	teaspoons baking powder
⅓	cup sugar	1½	cups milk
1	teaspoon salt	½	cup peanut butter

Preheat oven to 375 degrees. Combine dry ingredients. Add milk and peanut butter. Pour into one greased 8×4×3-inch loaf pan. Bake for approximately 50 minutes. Great with homemade jam.

Alberta DiClaudio, Savannah, GA

FRITTERS

1	egg, beaten	1	cup sour cream
½	cup milk	¼	cup vegetable oil
2	teaspoons sugar	3	pears, peeled,
1	teaspoon ground cinnamon		cored, and sliced
1	cup self-rising flour		horizontally

Combine beaten egg, milk, sugar, cinnamon, and flour. Mix well and add sour cream. Heat 2 tablespoons oil to 375 degrees. Dip pears in batter, carefully place in oil, and cook 1 to 2 minutes. Turn and cook 1 to 2 minutes more. Add oil as needed. Remove fritters and drain. May be sprinkled with powdered sugar or cinnamon sugar. Serve warm.

Diane Silver Berryhill, Savannah, GA

Breads

PENNSYLVANIA APPLESAUCE BREAD

Janet was kind enough to submit several of her own family's recipes *d*
to this cookbook. Thanks for sharing a part of your heritage with us.

2 cups all-purpose flour	1 teaspoon vanilla extract
¼ cup dark brown sugar	1 stick butter, softened
1 teaspoon baking powder	1 cup applesauce
1 teaspoon baking soda	2 eggs
¾ teaspoon salt	1 cup raisins
1 teaspoon ground cinnamon	½ cup chopped walnuts
½ teaspoon ground nutmeg	

Preheat oven to 350 degrees. Combine all ingredients except raisins and nuts. Mix well until blended. Stir in raisins and nuts. Pour into greased and floured 8×4×3-inch loaf pan. Bake for 60 to 65 minutes.

My mother, Alberta DiClaudio, was a great Pennsylvania Dutch cook and baker. My Italian father insisted that she feed him homemade everything. My brother and I benefited from her willingness to comply with his wishes. We enjoyed homemade breads, pastas, cakes, cookies, pies, and other desserts every day. The recipes included here are among her very best. Enjoy!   *Janet DiClaudio, Savannah, GA*

FRESH BLACKBERRY MUFFINS

1 stick butter, melted	2 teaspoons baking powder
½ cup milk	½ teaspoon salt
2 large eggs, at room temperature	2 cups fresh blackberries,
2 cups all-purpose flour	or frozen blackberries,
1¼ cups plus 4 teaspoons sugar	thawed and drained

Preheat oven to 350 degrees. Grease eighteen 2½-inch muffin tins, or line them with paper or foil liners. In a bowl, stir together butter, milk, and eggs. In a mixing bowl, sift together flour, 1¼ cups of the sugar, baking powder, and salt. Make a well in center of flour and pour in milk mixture all at once; stir until blended. Batter will be lumpy: Do not overmix. Fold in berries. Divide batter among prepared cups and sprinkle remaining 4 teaspoons of sugar over batter. Bake for about 25 minutes, or until golden.   *Kelley Ort, Atlanta, GA*

MOTHER'S ROLLS

½ cup Crisco shortening	1 package yeast
¼ cup sugar	½ cup lukewarm water
1 heaping teaspoon salt	1 egg
½ cup boiling water	3 cups sifted all-purpose flour

Cream together shortening, sugar, and salt. Add boiling water. Dissolve yeast in ½ cup lukewarm water; beat egg and add. Combine with shortening and mix all together with flour. Beat well. Set aside at room temperature for 30 minutes, then refrigerate until needed. Preheat oven to 350 degrees. Roll out dough and cut into rolls. Place on greased cookie sheet. Bake for 15 minutes or until brown. *Virginia Robertson, Albany, GA*

"RIZ BISCUITS"
My family has enjoyed many a wonderful meal in my brother and sister-in-law's home. We always look forward to Jill's marvelous biscuits.

1 ¼-ounce package dry yeast	1 teaspoon baking powder
1 cup warm buttermilk	¾ teaspoon salt
½ teaspoon baking soda	½ cup vegetable shortening
2½ cups all-purpose flour	Butter, melted
1 tablespoon sugar	

In a small bowl, dissolve yeast in buttermilk; add baking soda. In a mixing bowl, sift together flour, sugar, baking powder, and salt. Cut shortening into flour with a fork. Stir yeast mixture into flour mixture with a spoon. Dust a rolling pin with additional flour, and roll dough out thin; brush with melted butter. Fold dough into a double thickness and brush top with melted butter. Cut into rounds with a small biscuit cutter. Place rounds on a greased baking sheet and let rise for 1 hour. Preheat oven to 425 degrees. Bake biscuits for 10 to 12 minutes, or until lightly browned.

Jill Hiers, Albany, GA

HOT CAKES

2 eggs	1 cup buttermilk
2 tablespoons baking powder	½ teaspoon salt
1 tablespoon sugar	1 cup flour

Combine first five ingredients and beat well. Add enough flour to make a thin batter (usually about 1 cup). My favorite; fewer calories.

Virginia Robertson, Albany, GA

LADY WAFFLES

2¼ cups sifted flour	2 eggs, beaten
4 teaspoons baking powder	2¼ cups milk
¾ teaspoon salt	¾ cup salad oil
1½ tablespoons sugar	

Sift together dry ingredients. Combine eggs, milk, and oil. Add dry ingredients. Just before baking, beat only until dry ingredients are moist. Cook in waffle iron. *Delicious!!*

Jill Hiers, Albany, GA

PUMPKIN BREAD

4 eggs	1 cup chopped nuts
1 cup vegetable oil	3 cups sugar
⅔ cup water	2 teaspoons baking soda
1 1-pound can pumpkin	1½ teaspoons ground nutmeg
3½ cups all-purpose flour	1½ teaspoons ground cinnamon
Pinch of ground cloves (optional)	1½ teaspoons salt

Beat eggs; add oil, water, and pumpkin; mix well. Combine dry ingredients and add to pumpkin mixture; mix well. Pour into prepared loaf pans. Bake at 350 degrees for 1 hour, or until done. Let cool; remove from pans.

Jill Hiers, Albany, GA

PUMPKIN BREAD

3 cups sugar	2 teaspoons baking soda
1 cup vegetable oil	1½ teaspoons salt
4 eggs	1 teaspoon ground cinnamon
2 cups canned pumpkin	1 teaspoon ground nutmeg
⅔ cup water	½ to ¾ cup chopped pecans
3⅓ cups all-purpose flour	or walnuts

Preheat oven to 350 degrees. Grease and flour two loaf pans. Mix sugar and oil with mixer. Add eggs and blend. Add pumpkin and blend. Add water and blend. Combine remaining ingredients and add slowly. Fill pans equally and bake for 1 hour or until golden brown. *Variations:* For the oil, substitute ½ cup oil and add ½ cup applesauce. For banana bread, substitute 2 cups mashed, ripe bananas for pumpkin and omit nutmeg.

Kelley Ort, Atlanta, GA

CRACKLIN' CORN BREAD

1 cup cracklings	1 teaspoon salt
½ cup hot water	Small amount of cold water
2 cups sifted yellow cornmeal	Vegetable oil for skillet

Preheat oven to 425 degrees. Mash or break cracklings. Mix with hot water and pour into cornmeal; add salt. Use sufficient amount of cold water to make dough. Let stand 5 minutes. Shape into pones and place in a cast-iron skillet that has been heated with a few tablespoons of oil. Bake until brown, for about 15 minutes, then reduce heat to 350 degrees and bake for 30 to 45 minutes. The skillet should be placed near the top of the oven.

the Lady

EASY STREUSEL COFFEE CAKE

1 13-ounce package blueberry muffin mix	1 11-ounce can mandarin orange segments, drained

Preheat oven to 400 degrees. Grease 8-inch square pan. Prepare muffin batter as directed on package; pour into prepared pan. Arrange orange segments over batter. Sprinkle with streusel mixture. Bake at 400 degrees for 25 to 30 minutes. Cool; cut into squares. Makes 6 to 9 servings.

Streusel Mixture

¼ cup brown sugar, packed	¼ teaspoon ground cinnamon
3 tablespoons flour	2 tablespoons butter

Mix all ingredients together with fork until crumbly.

CHEESE BISCUITS

These biscuits have become one of our signature items at The Lady & Sons Restaurant. Everyone really looks forward to us bringing them out, whether it be after guests are seated or while they are waiting in line.

2 cups self-rising flour	¾ cup grated Cheddar cheese
1 teaspoon baking powder	1 cup buttermilk
1 teaspoon sugar	1 stick butter, melted
⅓ cup Crisco shortening	2 cloves garlic, crushed

Preheat oven to 350 degrees. Mix flour, baking powder, and sugar together using a fork; cut in shortening until it resembles cornmeal. Add cheese. Stir in buttermilk all at one time just until blended. Do not overstir. Drop by tablespoonfuls (I use an ice cream scoop to give biscuits a nicer shape) onto a well-greased baking sheet. Bake for 12 to 15 minutes. Makes 8 large biscuits. *Garlic Butter:* Combine butter and garlic over medium heat until butter absorbs garlic; brush over tops of warm biscuits. Store leftover butter for next baking. *Variation:* For breakfast, brush biscuits with plain butter or honey butter.

APPLESAUCE CUPCAKES

1 egg
2 cups all-purpose flour
½ teaspoon ground cloves
¼ teaspoon salt
1½ teaspoons ground nutmeg
1 teaspoon ground cinnamon
1½ sticks butter, melted

1 teaspoon vanilla extract
1 cup chopped pecans
1½ cups sugar
1 cup raisins
1½ cups hot applesauce
with 2 teaspoons baking
soda added

Preheat oven to 350 degrees. Mix above ingredients in bowl by hand except for applesauce. Last, add hot applesauce and baking soda. Pour batter into paper-lined cupcake pans. Bake for 25 minutes or until done.

the lady

LACE CORNBREAD

1 cup plain cornmeal
1 teaspoon salt

1½ cups water
Oil for frying

Combine ingredients and mix well. Batter will be very thin. Pour using a small ladle into a heavy skillet. Pan should be hot enough to make batter sizzle. Flip and brown on other side.

the lady

CORN BREAD

2 eggs
1¼ cups milk
¼ cup melted shortening
1½ cups plain cornmeal

¾ cup all-purpose flour
1 teaspoon salt
2½ teaspoons baking
powder

Preheat oven to 400 degrees. Beat eggs, add milk and shortening. Sift together remaining ingredients, add to egg mixture, beating well. Pour into greased shallow 9×9-inch pan. Bake about 20 to 25 minutes until edges pull away from sides of pan.

the lady

HOE CAKES

These hoe cakes are quickly becoming a favorite with our guests. They are almost as popular as our cheese biscuits. Use them to soak up that good pot liquor from our turnip greens. After the plate is completely sopped clean, save one to eat as a dessert along with table syrup.

1 cup self-rising flour	⅓ cup plus 1 tablespoon water
1 cup self-rising cornmeal	
2 eggs	¼ cup vegetable oil or bacon grease
1 tablespoon sugar	
¾ cup buttermilk	Oil or butter for frying

Mix all ingredients well except for frying oil. Heat oil in a skillet over medium heat. Drop mixture by tablespoonfuls into hot skillet. Use approximately 2 tablespoons batter per hoecake. Brown until crisp; turn and brown on other side. Drain on paper towels. Leftover batter will keep in refrigerator for up to 2 days.

EASY COFFEE CAKE

2 8-ounce cans refrigerated crescent rolls	1 teaspoon vanilla extract
1 cup sugar	1 egg, separated
2 8-ounce packages cream cheese, softened	½ cup chopped pecans

Preheat oven to 350 degrees. Spread one can of crescent rolls in bottom of 13×9-inch pan. Cream together ¾ cup sugar, cream cheese, vanilla, and egg yolk. Spread mixture over rolls. Top with second package of crescent roll dough. Beat egg white until frothy and spread on top. Sprinkle top with remaining sugar and nuts. Bake for 30 to 35 minutes.

Carolyn Cundiff, Athens, GA

Sauces, Soups Condiments & Relishes

House Seasoning

1 cup salt
1/4 cup black pepper
1/4 cup garlic

MOCHA SAUCE

½ cup unsweetened cocoa powder ½ cup honey
½ cup strong brewed coffee ¼ cup heavy cream

In a small saucepan, combine all ingredients and cook over medium heat, stirring constantly, until mixture is smooth and slightly thickened. Let cool. Makes 1 cup. *Diane Silver Berryhill, Savannah, GA*

OYSTER STEW

Susan and I have been like sisters for over 30 years, and we have broken many a piece of bread together. She is a great cook, and I think we are at our happiest when we are sharing meals together.

2 green onions, chopped 1 quart half-and-half or whole milk
2 tablespoons butter ¼ teaspoon salt
12 ounces fresh raw oysters, ¼ teaspoon white pepper
    undrained ⅛ teaspoon cayenne pepper

Sauté onion in butter until tender. Add remaining ingredients. Cook over low heat until edges of oysters begin to curl and mixture is hot but not boiling. Serve stew with crackers. Serves 4 to 5.

Susan Dupuy, Albany, GA

MAPLE SYRUP

1 cup water 1 cup brown sugar
1 cup white sugar ½ teaspoon maple flavoring

Mix water and sugars in a saucepan. Bring to a boil. Remove from heat, stir in maple flavoring, and store in refrigerator. *Sheila Mims, Albany, GA*

ASIAN MARINADE

½   cup soy sauce (lite)
¼   cup water
2   tablespoons vinegar
1   tablespoon vegetable oil

1   teaspoon sugar
¼   teaspoon ground ginger
    Garlic powder to taste

Combine all ingredients. Use with beef, chicken, or fish.

Denise Watson, Albany, GA

PEAR HONEY

1   20-ounce can crushed pineapple
    with syrup
1   tablespoon lemon juice

8   cups (about 3 pounds) peeled,
    cored, and chopped pears
10 cups sugar

Mix all ingredients and cook until pears are tender and mixture thickens, approximately 30 minutes. Place in sterilized jars and seal while still hot.

Jill Hiers, Albany, GA

MINT JULEP JELLY

1½ cups bourbon
½   cup water
3   cups sugar

6   tablespoons Certo
4 to 5 fresh mint sprigs

Combine bourbon, water, and sugar in double boiler over medium heat. Stir until sugar is dissolved. Remove from heat; add Certo. Pour into sterilized jars. Add mint sprig to each jar and seal.   *Jill Hiers, Albany, GA*

PORT WINE JELLY

1   cup port wine
1   cup cranberry juice

3½ cups sugar
½   bottle Certo

Stir wine, juice, and sugar together in double boiler over medium heat until sugar is dissolved. Remove from heat and add Certo. Pour into sterilized jars and seal immediately.   *Jill Hiers, Albany, GA*

STRAWBERRY FIG PRESERVES

3   cups mashed ripe figs
3   cups sugar

2   3-ounce packages strawberry
    Jell-O

Mix all ingredients together in saucepan and cook 4 minutes at rolling boil. Stir frequently. Skim. Pour into sterilized jars; seal. *Jill Hiers, Albany, GA*

PEPPER JELLY

¾   cup chopped green bell pepper
¼   cup chopped fresh hot green pepper
1½ cups apple vinegar

6   cups sugar
4   ounces Certo
4   drops green food coloring

Process bell and hot peppers in food processor, then mix in all ingredients except Certo and food coloring. Bring to rolling boil. Remove from heat and add Certo and coloring. Pour into sterilized jars and seal. *the Lady*

CHICKEN OR SHRIMP MARINADE

3   cloves garlic, crushed
1½ teaspoons salt
½   cup packed brown sugar
3   tablespoons Dijon mustard
¼   cup apple cider vinegar

6   tablespoons olive oil
    Juice of 1 lime
    Juice of ½ lemon
    Dash of cayenne or ground
    black pepper

Mix all ingredients with a whisk. Pour over chicken or shrimp. Refrigerate overnight. Grill over hot coals or broil in oven.

BARBECUE SAUCE

¼ cup vinegar
½ cup water
2 tablespoons mustard
½ teaspoon pepper
1½ teaspoons salt
1 tablespoon sugar

¼ teaspoon cayenne pepper
  Sliced lemon
  Sliced onion
¼ cup butter
½ cup catsup
2 tablespoons Worcestershire sauce

Mix first ten ingredients. Simmer 20 minutes uncovered. Add catsup and Worcestershire sauce; bring to a boil. Serve as desired.

Denise Watson, Albany, GA

LEMON COCKTAIL SAUCE

6 tablespoons mayonnaise
1 tablespoon horseradish
½ teaspoon grated onion

1 teaspoon prepared mustard
2 tablespoons lemon juice

Combine all ingredients and chill before serving. Makes ½ cup. Serve with cold shrimp, crab claws, or raw oysters.

BARBECUE SAUCE

Peggy Richardson is my Aunt Peggy's cousin. Their families have been intertwined for many years, and many good meals have been shared by the two of them.

1½ cups apple cider vinegar
1 to 2 tablespoons Worcestershire
  sauce
1 to 2 tablespoons peanut butter
1 teaspoon salt

  Juice of 2 lemons
1 teaspoon pepper
2 tablespoons celery seed
2 tablespoons chili powder
½ stick butter

Bring all ingredients to a boil until peanut butter dissolves. Stir to avoid sticking. Lower heat and simmer for 20 minutes.

Peggy Richardson, Albany, GA

SAUCE FOR GRILLED CHICKEN

½ cup distilled vinegar
½ cup lemon juice
½ cup corn oil
1 tablespoon salt

¼ teaspoon ground black pepper
1½ tablespoons dry mustard
Sprinkle of cayenne pepper

Mix ingredients together. Bring to boil over medium heat. Stir frequently.
Remove from heat; brush chicken with sauce while on the grill. Makes
enough sauce for 2 chickens.   *Denise Watson, Albany, GA*

EGG AND LEMON SAUCE

3 eggs, separated
   Juice of 2 lemons

1 tablespoon cornstarch
1 cup chicken stock

Beat egg whites until stiff; add egg yolks and continue beating. Add lemon
juice slowly. Beat constantly to prevent curdling. Dissolve cornstarch in
¼ cup water; add to broth and cook over medium heat until it thickens.
Slowly add hot stock to egg mixture, beating constantly. Sauce should
be smooth and creamy.   *the Lady*

GRAPE KETCHUP

Lorraine was very kind to share this recipe with us. She suggests this be served as a condiment with fried potatoes.

10	pounds fresh grapes	2	tablespoons ground cloves
2	quarts vinegar	1	grated nutmeg
5	pounds sugar	½	teaspoon salt
1	tablespoon ground cinnamon	1	teaspoon pepper
1	tablespoon ground allspice		

Pick over, remove stems from, wash, and drain grapes. Put in kettle, add cold water to barely cover, bring to a boiling point. Let simmer until fruit is soft; remove from heat. Press through a sieve, discarding skins and seeds. Put pulp into preserving kettle and add vinegar, sugar, spices, and seasonings. Bring to a boiling point and let simmer until reduced to the consistency of ketchup. Pour into sterilized jars and seal.

Lorraine Koenn, Savannah, GA

SHERRIED AVOCADO BOUILLON

2	10¾-ounce cans condensed beef broth	2	tablespoons chopped fresh parsley
1⅓	cups water		Salt and pepper to taste
¼	cup sherry	1	medium avocado, peeled and finely diced

Heat broth and water to boiling. Add sherry and parsley and season to taste with salt and pepper. Remove from heat and stir in avocado. Pour at once into heated bouillon cups. Garnish with avocado slices, if desired. Serves 6.

the lady

CHEESE SOUP

1	small onion, chopped	¾	cup grated sharp Cheddar cheese
2	large pimentos, chopped		Salt and ground black pepper
3	tablespoons butter		to taste
3	tablespoons all-purpose flour		Dash of cayenne pepper
1½	cups chicken stock		(optional)
1½	cups half-and-half		

In a saucepan, sauté onion and pimentos in butter for 5 to 7 minutes. Blend in flour. Add stock and half-and-half. Cook until thick. Add cheese and stir until melted. Add salt and black pepper to taste, and cayenne if desired.

the lady

BARBECUE SAUCE

½	cup oil	½	cup apple cider vinegar
¼	cup lemon juice	3	tablespoons Worcestershire
1	teaspoon pepper		sauce
¾	cup ketchup	2	teaspoons paprika
3	tablespoons brown sugar	¾	cup water
	Pinch of garlic salt or garlic	3	tablespoons prepared mustard
	powder	½	onion, finely chopped
2	teaspoons salt		

Mix all ingredients together and simmer over medium heat for 15 minutes.

the lady

SAUSAGE AND LENTIL SOUP

2	tablespoons olive oil	¾	teaspoon dried thyme
1	pound sausage (chorizo, Polish, etc.)	1	bay leaf
			8 to 9 cups chicken stock
7	ounces smoked ham, shredded	1	16-ounce can peeled tomatoes, crushed
2	large onions, chopped		
1	large green bell pepper, chopped	½	pound dried lentils (1¼ cups)
1	medium carrot, diced	12	large spinach leaves, cut into small pieces
2	cloves garlic, minced		
½	teaspoon ground cumin		Salt and pepper to taste

Heat olive oil in a large saucepan over medium heat. Add sausage and cook until done. Remove sausage and place on a platter, allowing time to cool. When cool, slice sausage into ⅛-inch slices. Discard all but 2 tablespoons of drippings from pan. Reheat drippings and add ham, onion, green pepper, and carrot to the saucepan. Cover and cook over medium heat for 15 minutes. Stir in garlic, cumin, thyme, and bay leaf. Cover and cook for 5 more minutes. Add chicken stock, sliced sausage, tomatoes, and lentils. Cover and cook over low heat for 2 hours. As soup cooks, skim off fat that rises to the top. After 2 hours turn off heat and discard bay leaf. Add spinach, salt, and pepper and let stand for 2 to 3 minutes before serving.   *Nancy Blood, Savannah, GA*

LEMON BUTTER FOR FISH

½	stick butter	Dash of Worcestershire sauce
1	clove garlic, minced	Salt and pepper to taste
2	tablespoons lemon juice	

Melt butter in a saucepan. Sauté garlic for 2 to 3 minutes. Add remaining ingredients and mix well. Serve warm over broiled fish.

LEMON BUTTER FOR STEAK

2   tablespoons lemon juice
3   tablespoons butter
¼   teaspoon salt

¼   teaspoon paprika
1   tablespoon finely chopped
    fresh parsley

Combine all ingredients. Pour over cooked
steaks and garnish with lemon wedges.

CREAM OF ARTICHOKE SOUP

2   13¾-ounce cans artichoke
    hearts, chopped
1½ cups chicken stock
1   cup chopped onion
½   stick butter

1   10¾-ounce can condensed
    cream of mushroom soup
⅓   cup heavy cream
    Salt and pepper to taste

Bring artichokes and chicken stock to a boil. In a saucepan, sauté onion
in butter and add to mixture. Gradually add mushroom soup to desired
thickness. Slowly add cream, stirring constantly. Remove from heat.
Add salt and pepper. Serves 6.

TOMATO DILL SOUP

3   cups peeled and diced fresh
    tomatoes (or one 28-ounce can)
1   medium onion, chopped
2   cups chicken stock
1   teaspoon chopped garlic
⅓ to ½ cup white wine
1   teaspoon lemon-pepper seasoning

3   tablespoons chopped fresh dill
¾   cup heavy cream
¼   cup chopped fresh parsley
¼   cup grated Parmesan cheese
    Salt and coarsely ground black
    pepper to taste

In a large pot, mix all ingredients together except heavy cream, parsley,
Parmesan, and salt and pepper. Cook over medium heat about 30 minutes,
until tomatoes are tender. Add cream, parsley, and Parmesan cheese.
Season with salt and pepper. Simmer for about 10 minutes.

Desserts

One More Candle & we're going to trigger the 5 ALARM FIRE Warning for Downtown Savannah!

CHOCOLATE POUND CAKE

3   cups sugar
2   sticks butter
½   cup vegetable shortening
5   eggs
3   cups all-purpose flour
4   tablespoons cocoa

½   teaspoon salt
½   teaspoon baking powder
½   teaspoon baking soda
1   cup buttermilk
1   tablespoon vanilla extract

Preheat oven to 350 degrees. Mix sugar with butter and vegetable shortening; add eggs one at a time, beating after each. Mix together dry ingredients. Add dry ingredients alternately with milk to butter mixture, beginning with flour and ending with flour. Add vanilla. Bake in a greased and floured tube pan for about 1 hour.   *Jessie R. Dixon, Eagle Lake, FL*

GRANDMAMA HIERS' PLAIN CAKE

½   pound butter
1⅔ cups sugar
5   eggs (6 if they are small)
2   cups all-purpose flour

Dash of salt
1½ tablespoons lemon juice
½   teaspoon almond
      flavoring

Cream butter and sugar. Add eggs, one at a time, beating well after each. Combine flour and salt; gradually add to mixture. Add lemon juice and almond flavoring. Pour into three 8-inch or two 9-inch cake pans. Bake at 325 degrees for 20 to 30 minutes. Cool. Frost with favorite frosting.
Jessie Dixon, Winter Haven, FL

LEMON GLAZE

Add 2 tablespoons lemon juice to 1 cup powdered sugar; stir until smooth. Brush over warm cookies or warm coffee cake. Also very good over pound cake.

GRANDMAMA HIERS' NEVER-FAIL POUND CAKE

My Grandmother Hiers was such a fine Christian woman, and my daddy adored her. Once when my daddy was very sick, he told me that his mother was truly an angel from God. She was only 4 feet 10 inches tall, and by the time I was 9 or 10 years old, I could wear her shoes. I could not wait to get to Grandmother Hiers' home so I could dress up in her high-heeled shoes.

3	sticks butter	3	cups cake flour
3	cups sugar	1	cup milk
5	eggs	2	teaspoons lemon extract

Cream butter and add sugar; gradually add eggs, one at a time, beating after each addition. Add flour and milk alternately; stir in lemon extract. Pour into a tube pan well sprayed with nonstick cooking spray. Bake at 325 degrees for 1 hour. Do not open oven door during baking. Pour lemon glaze over warm cake for a very delightful dessert.

the Lady

BANANA SPLIT CAKE

2	cups crushed graham crackers	1	20-ounce can crushed
3	sticks butter		pineapple, drained
2	eggs, or 2 pasteurized eggs	2 to 3	bananas, sliced
1	16-ounce box powdered sugar	1	12-ounce container Cool Whip

For crust, mix crushed graham crackers and 1 stick of butter. Line bottom and sides of a 13×9-inch pan with mixture. Beat until fluffy eggs, 2 sticks butter, and the powdered sugar. Spread mixture on crust. Add layer of crushed pineapple and layer of sliced bananas. Cover with Cool Whip. Sprinkle with nuts or graham crackers. Refrigerate for 1 hour.

Jessie R. Dixon, Eagle Lake, FL

GRANDMAMA HIERS' CARROT CAKE

2 cups all-purpose flour	4 eggs
2 cups sugar	1½ cups vegetable oil
2 teaspoons baking soda	3 cups grated carrots
2 teaspoons ground cinnamon	1½ cups chopped pecans (optional)
1 teaspoon salt	

Preheat oven to 350 degrees. In a large bowl, combine flour, sugar, baking soda, cinnamon, and salt. Add eggs and vegetable oil and mix well; add carrots and pecans. Pour into three 9-inch round greased, floured pans. Bake for approximately 40 minutes. Remove from oven and cool for 5 minutes. Remove from pans, place on waxpaper, and allow to cool completely before frosting.

Frosting

1 8-ounce package cream cheese	1 teaspoon vanilla extract
1 stick butter	½ cup chopped pecans
1 16-ounce box powdered sugar	

Combine all ingredients except for nuts and beat until fluffy. Stir in nuts. Frost cake. *Jessie R. Dixon, Eagle Lake, FL*

POUND CAKE

4 sticks butter	3 cups all-purpose flour
3 cups sugar	2 teaspoons vanilla extract
6 large eggs	

Cream butter and sugar. Add eggs, one at a time; beat 1 minute after each addition. Add flour and vanilla. Pour into greased and floured tube or Bundt pan. Do not preheat oven. Bake at 325 degrees for 85 minutes, or until done. *Sheila Mims, Albany, GA*

Another great Southwest Georgia cook, y'all!

CARROT CAKE

2	cups self-rising flour	1	cup Wesson oil
2	cups sugar	3	cups grated carrots
1½	teaspoons ground cinnamon	1	teaspoon vanilla extract
4	eggs	1	cup pecans, chopped

In a large bowl, combine flour, sugar, and cinnamon. Add eggs, one at a time, beating after each. Add vegetable oil and mix well; add carrots and vanilla. Add nuts last. Pour into greased, floured pans. Bake at 350 degrees approximately 40 minutes, or until done.

Frosting

1	cup sugar	½	teaspoon baking soda
2	tablespoons Karo syrup	1	teaspoon vanilla extract
½	cup buttermilk		

Mix sugar, syrup, and buttermilk; cook for 5 minutes. Add baking soda and vanilla and spread on cake.   *Mrs. Farley, Eagle Lake, FL*

GRANDMAMA HIERS' 1-2-3-4 CAKE

1	cup butter	3	cups cake flour
1	teaspoon vanilla extract	3	teaspoons baking powder
2	cups sugar	1	cup milk
4	eggs		

Cream butter, vanilla, and sugar; add eggs one at a time, beating after each. Combine cake flour and baking powder; add to creamed mixture, alternately with milk, beginning with flour and ending with flour. Mix well. Pour into two 9-inch pans or three 8-inch pans. Bake at 350 degrees for approximately 30 to 40 minutes, or until done.

Jessie R. Dixon, Eagle Lake, FL

THE ONLY LEMON CAKE

1	package lemon Jell-O	1	package Duncan Hines
¾	cup boiling water		yellow cake mix
¾	cup salad oil	1	tablespoon vanilla extract
4	eggs		

Mix above ingredients together and pour into a greased angel-food-cake pan. Bake at 350 degrees for 45 minutes. Remove from oven and let stand for 3 minutes. Turn out onto a cake plate, then prick top of cake with a fork or toothpick.

Icing

5	tablespoons lemon juice	Zest of 1 lemon
1½	cups powdered sugar	

Blend together in blender and pour over cake.

Alberta DiClaudio, Savannah, GA

LOW-FAT LEMONY CHEESECAKE WITH FRUIT

¼	cup graham cracker crumbs	⅓	cup ReaLemon lemon juice
2	8-ounce packages fat-free		from concentrate
	cream cheese	1	teaspoon vanilla extract
1	14-ounce can fat-free	⅓	cup unsifted flour
	sweetened condensed milk	1	cup assorted fruit,
4	whole eggs		for serving

Spray bottom and sides of 8-inch springform pan. Spread cracker crumbs in bottom of pan. In mixer bowl, beat cream cheese until fluffy. Gradually beat in condensed milk until smooth. Add eggs, lemon juice, and vanilla; mix well. Stir in flour. Pour into prepared pan. Bake 50 to 55 minutes, or until center is set. Cool. Serve chilled with fruit. Refrigerate leftovers.

Janet DiClaudio, Savannah, GA

MILLION-DOLLAR PIE

1 stick butter	1 quart heavy cream, whipped
1 cup all-purpose flour	with 1 cup sugar until stiff
½ cup chopped pecans	2 3.4-ounce packages instant
1 8-ounce package cream cheese	chocolate pudding mix
1 cup powdered sugar	3 cups milk

Preheat oven to 350 degrees. In a 13×9×2-inch glass dish, melt butter and stir in flour and ¼ cup of the nuts. Bake about 20 minutes, until firm. Let cool.

First layer: Combine cream cheese, powdered sugar, and 1 cup of whipped cream. Layer over cooked nut crust.

Second layer: Combine instant pudding mix and milk. Layer over first layer.

Third layer: Combine remaining whipped cream and remaining chopped nuts. Layer over top. Keep refrigerated.

the lady

AUNT GLENNIS' POUND CAKE

Aunt Glennis and Uncle Burney played a big part in my life.
For about 25 years, my whole family spent Thanksgivings in Statesboro.
The times we had were wonderful. We always looked forward to being
in their home. We lost Uncle Burney in 1996, and we will feel this loss
for a very long time.

½ cup Crisco shortening	1 cup milk
2 sticks butter	1 teaspoon vanilla extract
2¾ cups sugar	1 12-ounce package semisweet
6 large eggs	chocolate chips
3 cups all-purpose flour	1½ cups chopped pecans
1 teaspoon baking powder	or walnuts

Cream shortening, butter, and sugar. Add eggs, one at a time, beating
thoroughly after each. Sift flour with baking powder. Add to creamed
mixture, alternating with milk. Roll nuts and chocolate chips in a little
flour and add to mixture, then add vanilla. Pour into a greased and floured
tube pan. Place in cold oven and bake at 325 degrees for about 1½ hours,
or until done.   *Glennis Hiers, Statesboro, GA*

TUNNEL OF FUDGE CAKE

3 sticks butter	1 12-ounce can creamy
6 eggs	chocolate frosting
1½ cups sugar	2 cups chopped walnuts
2 cups all-purpose flour	or pecans

Preheat oven to 350 degrees. Cream butter in large bowl on high speed.
Add eggs one at a time, beating well. Add sugar gradually, creaming
at high speed, until light and fluffy. Gradually add flour. By hand, stir
in frosting mix and nuts until well blended. Pour batter in well-greased
and floured Bundt pan. Bake for 60 to 65 minutes. Cool 2 hours before
removing from pan. Cake will have a dry, brownie-type crust and a moist
center with a tunnel of fudge running through it.
Jacklyn Miller, Guyton, GA

DARK COCOA CAKE

1⅔ cups sugar
1 teaspoon vanilla extract
⅔ cup soft shortening
3 eggs
2¼ cups flour

⅔ cup cocoa
¼ teaspoon baking powder
1¼ teaspoons baking soda
1 teaspoon salt
1⅓ cups water

Cream sugar, vanilla, shortening, and eggs. Combine dry ingredients and blend into creamed mixture. Add water. Pour into 13×9-inch pan and bake at 350 degrees for approximately 40 minutes. Frost with favorite icing.

Alberta DiClaudio, Savannah, GA

PEACHY POUND CAKE

2 cups butter, at room temperature
2⅔ cups sugar
8 eggs, separated

3½ cups all-purpose flour, sifted
1 5½-ounce can evaporated milk
¾ cup peach preserves

Cream butter and 2 cups of the sugar. Beat until fluffy. Add egg yolks, one at time, beating after each. Alternately add flour and milk, beginning with flour and ending with flour. Beat egg whites with remaining sugar until stiff. Fold into batter. Pour batter into prepared tube pan; spoon preserves on top, 1 inch from outside edge of circle. Bake in cold oven at 300 degrees for 90 minutes.

the lady

CHOCOLATE CAKE

1 box Pillsbury fudge cake mix
1½ cups water
½ cup sour cream
4 eggs

1 8-ounce package cream cheese, softened
⅓ cup sugar
1 cup coconut

Combine cake mix with water, sour cream, and 2 slightly beaten eggs. Beat as directed on the box. Pour half of the batter into a tube pan or a 13×9-inch loaf pan. In a small bowl, combine softened cream cheese with remaining 2 eggs, sugar, and coconut. Pour over batter in pan. Cover with remaining batter. Bake at 350 degrees for 35 to 40 minutes. Frost with cream-cheese icing.   *Alberta DiClaudio, Savannah, GA*

BUTTERMILK POUND CAKE

3 cups sugar
1 cup shortening
5 eggs, separated, egg whites well beaten
1 teaspoon vanilla extract

1 cup buttermilk
¼ teaspoon baking soda
3 cups cake flour
½ cup grated coconut (optional)

Cream sugar and shortening; add egg yolks and vanilla, beating well. Add ½ cup of the buttermilk with baking soda dissolved in it. Add flour and remaining buttermilk. Mix well. Fold in beaten egg whites. Pour into greased and floured tube pan. Bake at 325 degrees for 1½ hours. Cool 10 minutes before removing from pan, and if you like, sprinkle with coconut.   *the Lady*

LEMON CHEESECAKE

1½ sticks butter	1 cup milk
2 cups sugar	1 teaspoon vanilla extract
3½ cups all-purpose flour	6 egg whites, beaten
3½ teaspoons baking powder	to stiff peaks

Preheat oven to 375 degrees. Cream butter; add sugar. Sift flour and baking powder together three times and add to butter alternately with milk and vanilla. Fold in egg whites. Bake in three greased 8-inch round pans for 35 minutes.

Icing

9 egg yolks	3 sticks butter
1½ cups sugar	Juice and zest of 4 lemons

Mix all ingredients together and cook in double boiler until thick, approximately 20 minutes. Allow cake to cool. Spread icing in between layers and on entire outside of cake.

the Lady

119

ORANGE SLICE CAKE

Cake

4	cups all-purpose flour
1½	teaspoons baking soda
1	pound candy orange slices, cut into small pieces
1	8-ounce package pitted dates, cut into small pieces
2	cups chopped pecans
1	cup shredded coconut

2	sticks butter
2	cups granulated sugar
4	eggs
½	cup buttermilk

Glaze

1	cup powdered sugar
2	tablespoons orange juice
1	teaspoon grated orange zest

Preheat oven to 300 degrees. Grease a 10-inch tube pan. For the cake, in a medium bowl, sift together 3½ cups of the flour and ½ teaspoon of the baking soda. In another bowl, mix orange slices, dates, and remaining ½ cup flour. Add nuts and coconut; set aside. In a large bowl, cream butter and sugar. Add eggs and beat well. In a small bowl, stir remaining 1 teaspoon baking soda into buttermilk. Alternately add flour mixture and buttermilk mixture to egg mixture, beginning and ending with flour. Fold in candy mixture. Pour batter into prepared pan and bake for 1¾ to 2 hours, or until a wooden pick inserted in center comes out clean. Cool cake in pan for 10 minutes, then turn out onto rack. To make glaze, stir together powdered sugar, orange juice, and zest. Drizzle glaze over warm cake. *the lady*

CRACKER CAKE

6	egg whites
2	cups sugar
1	teaspoon vanilla extract
1½	cups soda crackers, crushed

2	cups nuts
2	teaspoons baking powder
1	14½-ounce can cherry pie filling
	Cool Whip

Beat egg whites until stiff; add sugar and vanilla. Combine crackers, nuts, and baking powder; add to egg-white mixture. Pour into a 13×9-inch pan lined with parchment paper and bake at 325 degrees for 40 to 45 minutes. Cool, spread with cherry pie filling, and top with Cool Whip.

Alberta DiClaudio, Savannah, GA

MAMA'S POUND CAKE

My mama was my dearest friend in all the world. I lost my mother when I was 23. What a privilege it was to know her and to call this lady "mother." I only wish I could have had more years to spend with her.

2	sticks butter	½	teaspoon salt
½	cup Crisco shortening	½	teaspoon baking powder
3	cups sugar	1	cup milk
5	eggs	1	teaspoon vanilla extract
3	cups all-purpose flour		

Preheat oven to 325 degrees. Cream butter and shortening together. Add sugar, a little at a time. Add eggs, one at a time, beating after each. Sift together dry ingredients and add to mixture alternately with milk, starting with flour and ending with flour. Add vanilla. Pour into greased and floured tube pan and bake for 1½ hours.

the lady

POUND CAKE

2	sticks butter, softened	½	teaspoon baking powder
½	cup shortening, softened	1	cup milk
3	cups sugar	1	teaspoon vanilla extract
5	large eggs	1	teaspoon lemon
3	cups plain all-purpose flour		flavoring

Cream butter and shortening; add sugar, beating until smooth. Add eggs one at a time, beating after each. Combine flour and baking powder and add to egg mixture alternately with milk; add flavorings. Pour into a large greased tube pan. Bake at 325 degrees for 75 minutes.

Jill Hiers, Albany, GA

GRANDMOTHER PAUL'S SOUR CREAM POUND CAKE
*My dear Grandmother Paul's impact on my life leaves me at a
loss for words, but it was her influence that set me on my path in life.*

2	sticks butter	½	teaspoon baking soda
3	cups sugar	6	eggs
1	cup sour cream	1	teaspoon vanilla extract
3	cups all-purpose flour		

Preheat oven to 325 degrees. Cream butter and sugar together; add sour
cream. Sift flour and baking soda together. Add to creamed mixture,
alternately with eggs, one at a time, beating after each. Add vanilla. Pour
into a greased and floured tube pan and bake for 1 hour 20 minutes.

the Lady

MILKY WAY ICE CREAM

1½	cups sugar	2	teaspoons vanilla extract
6	eggs, well beaten	1	can condensed milk
2	large cans evaporated milk	1	pint whipping cream
8	Milky Way bars, chopped	1	pint half-and-half

Beat sugar and eggs, adding one at a time, beating well after each addition.
Add evaporated milk; cook over medium heat, stirring constantly. Cook
until mixture coats a spoon. Remove from heat; add chopped candy bars,
vanilla, and condensed milk. Pour into 1-gallon freezer container; stir in
whipping cream and half-and-half. If necessary, add milk to finish filling
container to within 2 inches of top. Freeze according to freezer directions.

Denise Watson, Albany, GA

CHOCOLATE POUND CAKE WITH ICING

½ cup shortening
2 sticks butter
2½ cups sugar
5 eggs
3 cups all-purpose flour

½ teaspoon baking powder
1 teaspoon salt
½ cup Nestlé Quik
1 cup milk

Cream shortening, butter, and sugar; add eggs one at a time. Mix flour, baking powder, and salt with Nestlé Quik. Add to egg mixture, alternating with milk, beginning with flour mixture and ending with flour mixture. Bake at 325 degrees for 80 minutes.

Icing

½ stick butter, melted
⅓ cup Nestlé Quik chocolate
⅓ cup milk

Vanilla extract, as desired
1 to 1½ boxes 10X powdered sugar
Pecan halves (optional)

Mix butter, chocolate, and milk until smooth. Add vanilla. Add sugar until consistency for spreading on cake. Add pecan halves to top of cake if desired.   *Pat Coppage, Savannah, GA*

AUNT GLENNIS' CHEWY CAKE

3 eggs
1 stick butter
1 box light brown sugar
2 cups self-rising flour
1 tablespoon vanilla extract

2 cups chopped nuts
1 cup coconut (optional)
1 small package semisweet
   chocolate chips

Beat eggs and butter together; add brown sugar. Gradually add flour; mix well. Stir in vanilla. Fold in nuts, coconut (if desired), and chocolate chips. Bake in a greased and floured 13×9-inch sheet pan at 375 degrees for 25 to 30 minutes. Cool and cut into squares.

Glennis Hiers, Statesboro, GA

My Uncle Burney's wife deserves a diamond in her crown for putting up with all us Hiers all these years.

RED VELVET CAKE

1½ cups vegetable oil	2½ cups cake flour
1½ cups sugar	1 teaspoon baking soda
2 eggs	1 cup buttermilk
1 teaspoon vinegar	1 1⅝-ounce bottle red food
1 teaspoon vanilla extract	coloring

Beat oil and sugar together. Blend in eggs, vinegar, and vanilla. Sift together flour and baking soda. Add to creamed mixture. Blend well. Add buttermilk and food coloring. Beat well. Will make 3 layers. Bake at 350 degrees for 25 minutes.

Filling and Icing

1 8-ounce package cream cheese	1 cup chopped nuts
1 box confectioners sugar	1 teaspoon vanilla extract
1 stick butter	

Allow ingredients to set at room temperature. Blend well and spread on cooled cake.
Denise Watson, Albany, GA

CHOCOLATE CHIP COOKIES AND CREAM

Ever had unexpected company drop in? Try this for a tasty quick dessert that's good served along with a cup of coffee. This can be chocolate chip or any kind of cookie, for that matter.

You will need 1 cup of milk, one 13-ounce package of chocolate chip cookies (or fresh-baked cookies), and 2 cups fresh whipping cream or Cool Whip—I prefer fresh-whipped cream.

Pour milk into a bowl; place cookies in milk, allowing them to soak for a minute or two. Alternate layers in a serving dish with cookies and cream; beginning with cream and ending with cream.

Variations: Try whipping cream with a flavoring such as vanilla, rum, almond, or chocolate cocoa. For additional ideas, see "Secrets from The Lady," on page xii. Enjoy!

CHOCOLATE SHEET CAKE

2	cups sugar	¼	cup cocoa
½	teaspoon salt	2	eggs
2	cups all-purpose flour	1	teaspoon baking soda
1	stick butter	½	cup buttermilk
½	cup vegetable oil	1	teaspoon vanilla extract
1	cup water		

Preheat oven to 350 degrees. Combine sugar, salt, and flour in a large mixing bowl. In a saucepan, bring to a boil butter, oil, water, and cocoa. Add to flour mixture. Beat eggs, baking soda, buttermilk, and vanilla. Add to dry ingredients. Pour into greased and floured 13×9×2-inch pan. Bake for 25 minutes.

Icing

1	stick butter	1	teaspoon vanilla extract
3	tablespoons cocoa	1	16-ounce box powdered sugar
6	tablespoons milk	1	cup chopped pecans or walnuts

Melt together butter and cocoa. Add milk and vanilla. Stir in powdered sugar and nuts. Spread on warm cake. *the lady*

CANDIED FRUIT CAKE

1	pound dates	2	teaspoons baking powder
1	pound candied pineapple	½	teaspoon salt
1	pound candied cherries	4	eggs
2	pounds nuts (about 8 cups)	1	cup sugar
2	cups flour		

Chop dates, pineapple, cherries, and nuts. Sift together flour, baking powder, and salt; dredge fruit and nuts in flour mixture. Beat eggs well; add sugar. Pour over dredged fruit and mix well. Bake in paper-lined pan at 275 degrees for 75 minutes, or until done. Makes about 5 pounds. *the lady*

GRANDMOTHER PAUL'S RED VELVET CAKE

2 eggs	1 teaspoon salt
2 cups sugar	1 cup buttermilk
1 teaspoon cocoa	1 teaspoon vanilla extract
2 ounces red food coloring	½ teaspoon baking soda
2 sticks butter	1 tablespoon vinegar
2½ cups cake flour	

Preheat oven to 350 degrees. Beat eggs; add sugar. Mix cocoa and food coloring. Add butter and egg mixture; mix well. Sift together flour and salt. Add to creamed mixture alternately with buttermilk. Blend in vanilla. In a small bowl, combine soda and vinegar and add to mixture. Pour into three 9-inch round greased and floured pans. Bake for 20 to 25 minutes, or until tests done.

Icing

2 egg whites	1 cup miniature marshmallows
1½ cups sugar	1 cup or 3½-ounce can shredded
5 tablespoons cold water	coconut
2 tablespoons light corn syrup	1 cup chopped pecans

Cook egg whites, sugar, water, and corn syrup in double boiler for 5 minutes and beat. Add marshmallows; stir until melted. Fold in coconut and nuts. Spread between layers and on top and sides of cooled cake.

the Lady

126

GOOEY BUTTER CAKES

I could write a full chapter on this dessert. It is the number-one choice in our restaurant. This recipe was given to me several years ago. While it is quite delicious, I wanted to come up with different variations. We have taken this one gooey butter cake recipe and have adapted it for just about any occasion. Below are additional variations that we have used. If you come up with something different, share your ideas with us.

1	18¼-ounce package yellow cake mix	1	egg
		1	stick butter, melted

Preheat oven to 350 degrees. Combine ingredients and mix well. Pat into a lightly greased 13×9-inch baking pan. Prepare filling.

Filling

1	8-ounce package cream cheese, softened	1	teaspoon vanilla extract
2	eggs	1	stick butter, melted
		1	16-ounce box powdered sugar

Beat cream cheese until smooth. Add eggs and vanilla. Add butter; beat. Add powdered sugar and mix well. Spread over cake mixture. Bake for 40 to 50 minutes. You want the center to be a little gooey, so do not overbake.

Variations

1. For the holidays, add a 15-ounce can of pumpkin to the filling; add ground cinnamon and ground nutmeg.

2. Add a 20-ounce can of drained crushed pineapple to the filling.

3. Use a lemon cake mix. Add lemon juice and zest to the filling.

4. Use a chocolate cake mix with cream cheese filling. Add chocolate chips and nuts on top.

5. Use a spiced carrot cake mix. Add chopped nuts and shredded carrots to the filling.

6. Use mandarin oranges, bananas, blueberries, or strawberries — just coordinate your extract flavorings.

7. Use a chocolate cake mix. Add ¾ to 1 cup peanut butter and nuts to the filling.

the lady

COCONUT CAKE

As an adult I returned to school; and although I was studying communications, I used this recipe as my class project discussion, not knowing it was my destiny to become a restaurant owner.

1   18¼-ounce package yellow
pudding cake mix
1   cup sour cream

1½ cups sugar
12 ounces canned or frozen
shredded coconut

Preheat oven to 350 degrees. Make cake by following directions on package, substituting milk for water. Divide and bake in three 9-inch round cake pans for 20 minutes. Remove from oven and allow to cool for 5 minutes. Remove from pans. Stir together sour cream, sugar, and coconut. Spread between slightly warm cake layers, piercing each layer as you stack them. Store cake in container in refrigerator for 2 to 3 days. This allows cake to soak up moisture from the coconut. On the third day, prepare icing for cake.

Icing

2   unbeaten egg whites
1½ cups sugar
2   teaspoons light corn syrup,
or ¼ teaspoon cream of tartar
⅓   cup cold water

Dash of salt
1   teaspoon vanilla extract
Additional coconut to
top icing (about ½ cup)

Place all ingredients except vanilla and additional coconut in top of double boiler, but do not place over heat; beat 1 minute with electric hand mixer. Place over boiling water and cook, beating constantly, until frosting forms stiff peaks (about 7 minutes). Remove from boiling water; add vanilla and beat until it reaches spreading consistency (about 2 minutes). Frost top and sides of cake; sprinkle with additional coconut. Cover and store at room temperature.

the lady

PISTACHIO CAKE

1 15¼-ounce Duncan Hines buttery cake mix	4 eggs
1 3-ounce box pistachio instant pudding mix	½ pint sour cream (low fat)
	¼ cup canola oil
	½ cup water

Combine cake mix and pudding mix. Add eggs, one at time; add sour cream, oil, and water. Mix well. Pour half of the batter into a greased tube pan. Add filling, top with remaining batter, and bake at 350 degrees for 55 minutes.

Filling

½ cup chopped nuts   1 tablespoon ground cinnamon
4 tablespoons sugar

Mix ingredients together and add to center of cake. Add powdered-sugar-and-milk glaze, if desired.   *Janet DiClaudio, Savannah, GA*

APPLE CAKE

⅔ cup vegetable oil   1 teaspoon baking soda
2 cups sugar   ¼ teaspoon salt
2 eggs   2 teaspoons ground cinnamon
2 teaspoons vanilla extract   4 large apples, peeled and sliced
2 cups all-purpose flour   1 cup chopped walnuts

Cream oil, sugar, and eggs; add vanilla; beat until creamy. Sift together flour, baking soda, salt, and cinnamon and add to creamed mixture. Fold in apples and nuts. Pour into sheet pan and bake at 350 degrees for 45 to 60 minutes.

Icing

2 cups powdered sugar   1 8-ounce package cream cheese
1½ tablespoons melted butter   ½ cup chopped walnuts

Cream sugar, butter, and cream cheese together until smooth; fold in nuts. Spread on cake.   *the lady*

129

GRANDMOTHER PAUL'S JAPANESE FRUIT CAKE

4	eggs	2	teaspoons baking powder
2	cups sugar	1	teaspoon salt
1	cup shortening	1	cup milk
3	cups all-purpose flour	1	teaspoon vanilla extract

Spray three 8-inch diameter cake pans with nonstick cooking spray. Beat eggs; add sugar and shortening. Sift dry ingredients together and add, alternately with milk, to the egg mixture. Add vanilla. Pour 1¾ cups batter each into two of the prepared pans. Into the remaining batter, add the following after tossing them together gently:

1	teaspoon ground cinnamon	½	cup raisins,
½	teaspoon ground cloves		dredged in flour
1	teaspoon ground allspice	½	cup nuts

Pour spiced batter into third prepared pan and bake all three layers at 325 degrees for 25 to 30 minutes. Put spiced layer in center when layering cake.

Filling

2	cups sugar	1	large can crushed
1	can grated coconut, drained		pineapple, drained
1	cup boiling water		Juice and zest of
2	tablespoons cornstarch mixed		two lemons
	in small amount of cold water		

Mix together and cook until thick enough to spread on cake layers. *Variation:* Stir in maraschino cherries cut in half.

the Lady

RUM CAKE

1 cup chopped walnuts	4 eggs
1 18¼-ounce package yellow cake mix	½ cup buttermilk
	½ cup vegetable oil
1 3½-ounce package instant vanilla pudding mix	½ cup dark rum

Preheat oven to 325 degrees. Grease and flour a 10-inch tube pan. Sprinkle nuts over bottom of pan. Mix remaining ingredients together. Pour batter over nuts. Bake for 1 hour. Cool. Invert on service plate. Prick top with fork or toothpick. Drizzle and smooth glaze evenly over top and sides. Allow cake to absorb glaze. Use all the glaze.

Glaze

½ stick butter	1 cup sugar
¼ cup water	½ cup dark rum

Melt butter in saucepan. Stir in water and sugar. Boil 5 minutes, stirring constantly. Remove from heat; stir in rum.

the lady

ICEBOX FRUIT CAKE

1 can sweetened condensed milk	2 cups chopped pecans
1 10-ounce bag marshmallows	1 pound chopped dates
1 14.4-ounce box graham crackers, crushed	1 10-ounce jar maraschino cherries, drained
1 7-ounce bag shredded coconut	

Heat condensed milk and melt marshmallows. Combine graham crackers, coconut, pecans, and dates. Fold in cherries and marshmallow mixture; mix well. Pour into 16×9-inch Pyrex dish and refrigerate for 1 hour or more. Cut into ½- to 1-inch slices; serve.

the lady

HAWAIIAN PINEAPPLE CAKE

1 16-ounce can crushed pineapple in heavy syrup	¾ cup sour cream
	1 stick butter
2 cups Bisquick	2 teaspoons vanilla extract
1 cup sifted all-purpose flour	2 large eggs
1 teaspoon baking soda	2 tablespoons rum
1 cup sugar	

Preheat oven to 350 degrees. Drain pineapple well, reserving syrup for glaze. Stir Bisquick, flour, and baking soda together and set aside. Beat sugar, sour cream, butter, and vanilla together for 2 minutes. Add eggs and beat 1 additional minute. Add flour mixture and beat 1 minute longer. Mix in drained pineapple and rum. Pour into well-greased 9-inch Bundt pan. Bake for about 45 minutes, or until cake tests done. Remove from oven and spoon about half the glaze over cake. Let stand 10 minutes and then turn onto serving plate. Spoon on remaining glaze. Cool before cutting.

Glaze

¾ cup sugar	¼ cup reserved pineapple syrup
4 tablespoons butter	2 tablespoons rum (optional)

Combine sugar, butter, and syrup. Stir over low heat until sugar is dissolved and butter is melted. Remove from heat and add rum, if desired.

the lady

EASY FRUIT CAKE

2 cups sugar	1 teaspoon lemon extract
1 pound candied pineapple	1 cup plain flour
1 pound candied cherries	1 cup self-rising flour
6 eggs	1 quart pecans
2 sticks butter	1 cup coconut
1 teaspoon vanilla extract	

Pour sugar over pineapple and cherries; let stand. Beat eggs, butter, and flavorings together. Combine plain and self-rising flour, and add sugared fruit; combine with egg mixture. Fold in pecans and coconut. Pour into greased tube pan and bake at 300 degrees for 2 hours, or until cake tests for doneness.

TONI'S FRESH-COCONUT CAKE

1 cup shortening	¼ teaspoon salt
2 cups sugar	3 teaspoons baking powder
4 eggs, separated	1 cup milk
3 cups sifted all-purpose flour	1 teaspoon vanilla extract

Cream shortening and sugar; add egg yolks, one at a time, beating after each. Sift dry ingredients together and add to mixture, alternately with milk. Add vanilla. Beat egg whites and fold into mixture. Bake at 350 degrees until done. Remove from oven, pierce layers with fork or toothpick so icing can penetrate. Makes three 8-inch layers.

Icing

3 fresh coconuts	4 tablespoons cornstarch
4 cups sugar	

Open coconuts and reserve milk. Peel and grate coconuts. In saucepan, mix sugar and cornstarch and add milk from coconuts. Boil for 12 minutes. Frost cake, alternating with grated coconut. The flavor is enhanced if you freeze this cake for several days before serving. *To freeze:* Wrap lightly in foil.

AUNT MYRTLE'S AMALGAMATION CAKE

2	cups sugar	4	cups flour, sifted
1½	cups shortening	6	eggs
1	cup buttermilk	1	tablespoon ground
2	teaspoons baking soda		cinnamon

Combine all ingredients; mix well. Pour into three greased and floured 8-inch round cake pans. Bake at 350 degrees until tests done.

Filling

5	egg yolks	1	cup pecans, ground
1	cup butter	1	cup raisins, ground
2	cups sugar	1	cup coconut, ground

Mix egg yolks, butter, and sugar in a double boiler and cook until thick. Remove from heat and add other ingredients; cool. Spread on cake. *Variations:* Use dates in lieu of raisins; chop instead of grind. Use filling between layers only and frost with Seven-Minute Icing.

Jean Gregory, Brunswick, GA

RESA'S CHOCOLATE STRAWBERRY SHORTCAKE

2 cups cake flour
1½ cups sugar
⅔ cup cocoa
½ cup Crisco shortening
1½ cups buttermilk
1½ teaspoons baking soda

1 teaspoon salt
1 teaspoon vanilla extract
2 whole eggs or 3 egg whites
1 quart fresh strawberries,
  rinsed and sliced
1 cup whipped cream or Cool Whip

Preheat oven to 350 degrees. In a mixing bowl, combine all ingredients in order listed, except strawberries and whipping cream. Beat with mixer on low speed, scraping bowl constantly, for 30 seconds. Beat on high speed, scraping bowl occasionally, for 3 minutes. Pour into greased and floured 13×9-inch pan. Bake for 30 to 35 minutes. Cool cake completely. Cut into squares. Place 2 or 3 squares in dessert cups and layer with small amount of strawberries and whipped cream. Garnish with strawberries. *A heavenly treat!*   *Resa Creo, Savannah, GA*

LUSCIOUS LIME CHEESECAKE

1 18¼-ounce package yellow
  cake mix
4 eggs
¼ cup vegetable oil
2 8-ounce packages cream
  cheese, at room temperature
1 14-ounce can sweetened
  condensed milk

2 teaspoons grated lime zest
⅓ cup fresh lime juice
1 teaspoon vanilla extract
1 8-ounce container Cool
  Whip, or 2 cups heavy cream,
  whipped with ½ cup sugar
  until stiff
  Lime slices, for garnish

Preheat oven to 300 degrees. Reserve ½ cup dry cake mix. In large bowl, combine remaining cake mix, 1 egg, and oil. Mix well (mixture will be crumbly). Press evenly in bottom and 1½ inches up sides of greased 13×9-inch pan. In same bowl, beat cheese until fluffy. Beat in condensed milk until smooth. Add remaining eggs and reserved cake mix and beat 1 minute at medium speed. Stir in lime zest, lime juice, and vanilla. Pour into prepared crust. Bake for 50 to 55 minutes, or until center is firm. Cool to room temperature. Chill thoroughly. Spread Cool Whip over top. Cut into squares to serve. Garnish with lime slices.

LUSCIOUS LOW-FAT PEACH CAKE

¼ teaspoon sugar
1 teaspoon ground cinnamon

Cake
2 cups all-purpose flour
1½ cups sugar
½ cup Crisco shortening
½ cup milk

1 15-ounce can cling peaches, drained (reserve ½ cup juice)
3 egg whites
3½ teaspoons baking powder
½ teaspoon ground cinnamon
1 teaspoon vanilla extract
1 teaspoon salt

Preheat oven to 350 degrees. Use nonstick cooking spray in Bundt pan. Mix together sugar and cinnamon. Sprinkle mixture over bottom and sides of pan. Combine all cake ingredients together, including reserved juice. Beat with mixer on low speed for 30 seconds, scraping bowl constantly. Beat on high speed for 2 minutes. Pour into Bundt pan. Bake for 40 to 45 minutes. Remove from oven; cool completely. Frost with icing immediately before serving.

Icing

1 6-ounce container nonfat peach yogurt

1 8-ounce container Lite Cool Whip

Mix together. Frost cake.

Resa Creo, Savannah, GA

GRANDMAMA HIERS' BUTTERNUT CAKE

2	cups sugar	½	tablespoon butter extract
1	cup Crisco	4	eggs
½	tablespoon almond or pecan extract	2	cups self-rising flour
		1	cup milk

Cream sugar and Crisco; add extracts and eggs, one at a time, beating after each addition. Add flour and milk alternately, beginning with flour and ending with flour. Pour into three greased and floured 8-inch cake pans. Bake at 350 degrees for 25 to 30 minutes. Stack cakes and frost with butternut icing while warm.

Icing

1	8-ounce package cream cheese	½	tablespoon almond or pecan extract
1	stick butter		
1	box powdered sugar	1	cup chopped pecans
½	tablespoon butter extract		

Combine first five ingredients and mix well. Fold in nuts.

Aunt Trina Bearden, Houma, LA

TURTLE CAKE

3	large eggs	1	14-ounce package caramels
1	cup water	1	stick butter
⅓	cup oil	1	can sweetened condensed milk
1	16½-ounce box German chocolate cake mix	6	ounces semisweet chocolate chips
		1	cup walnuts

Using eggs, water, and oil, prepare German chocolate cake mix according to directions on box. Spray a 16×9-inch cake pan with nonstick cooking spray and add one-half of the batter. Reserve the other half for later. Bake at 350 degrees for 15 minutes. Remove from heat; cool completely.

Melt caramels and butter. When completely melted, remove from heat and stir in condensed milk until smooth. Let mixture cool completely. Add chocolate chips and walnuts and blend. Spread over cooled cake. Pour remaining cake batter on top and return to 350-degree oven for another 20 to 25 minutes. Cool and cut into squares. This cake freezes well for up to 3 months.

Susan Dupuy, Albany, GA

WALNUT RUM CAKE

1 15¼-ounce package yellow cake mix (*not* with pudding mix)	¾ cup water
	1 5.1-ounce package instant vanilla pudding mix
1 cup walnuts, chopped	4 eggs
½ cup oil	Whipped cream, for serving

Coat tube pan with nonstick spray and dust with flour. Mix above and bake at 350 degrees for 60 minutes. Remove from heat and prick all over with basting fork. Drizzle sauce over. *Variations:* Bourbon can be substituted for rum. Pecans can be substituted for walnuts.

Sauce

½ stick butter, melted	½ cup dark rum
½ cup sugar	

Heat all until sugar is melted, then drizzle over warm cake. When completely cool, turn out on cake plate. Reheat at 200 degrees for 20 minutes before serving. Serve warm with whipped cream.

Susan Dupuy, Albany, GA

ITALIAN LOVE CAKE

Cake

		Icing	
2 pounds ricotta cheese		1 5.1-ounce package instant chocolate pudding mix	
4 eggs			
¾ cup sugar		1 cup cold milk	
1 teaspoon vanilla extract		8 ounces Cool Whip	
1 package fudge marble cake mix			

Preheat oven to 350 degrees. Grease and flour a 13×9-inch pan. For the cake, in a medium bowl, mix ricotta cheese, eggs, sugar, and vanilla; set aside. Prepare cake mix according to package directions and pour batter into prepared pan. Immediately spread ricotta mixture directly on top. Bake for 1 hour. Remove from oven and let cool completely in pan. For the icing, in a medium bowl, stir pudding mix into milk, then fold in Cool Whip. Spread icing on cake in pan and refrigerate overnight.

Resa Creo, Savannah, GA

BOSTON FUDGE CAKE WITH FUDGE SAUCE

2	cups brown sugar	3	eggs
½	cup Crisco shortening	2	cups sifted all-purpose flour
1	cup buttermilk	1	teaspoon baking soda
1	teaspoon vanilla extract	½	teaspoon salt
2	ounces unsweetened chocolate, melted		

Preheat oven to 350 degrees. Cream together brown sugar and shortening; add buttermilk and vanilla. Add melted chocolate, then add eggs one at a time; beat for 2 minutes. Sift together flour, baking soda, and salt and add to creamed mixture. Beat an additional 2 minutes. Pour into a 13×9×2-inch greased, floured pan. Bake for 40 to 45 minutes.

Hot Fudge Sauce
Also excellent poured over individual servings of your favorite sheet cake.

1	4-ounce bar German chocolate	3	cups powdered sugar
½	ounce unsweetened chocolate	1⅔	cups evaporated milk
1	stick butter	1¼	teaspoons vanilla extract

Melt chocolate and butter in saucepan over very low heat. Stir in powdered sugar, alternating with evaporated milk, blending well. Bring to a boil over medium heat, stirring constantly. Cook and stir until mixture becomes thick and creamy, about 8 minutes. Stir in vanilla; serve warm over Savannah Chocolate Cake (or your favorite sheet cake). Makes 3 cups.

ICEBOX CAKE

1 15¼-ounce box Duncan Hines yellow cake mix	1 cup water
½ cup oil	1 3.4-ounce package vanilla instant pudding
3 eggs	

Beat all ingredients for 2 or 3 minutes. Pour into 13×9×2-inch pan. Bake at 350 degrees for 35 to 40 minutes. Pour following icing over warm cake and refrigerate for 2 days.

Icing

1½ cups sugar
1 8-ounce package sour cream
1 7-ounce bag shredded coconut

1 small can crushed pineapple, drained

Mix above with an electric mixer. Pour over warm cake.   *the lady*

GOLDEN-GLOW SOUR CREAM CAKE

2 sticks butter
3 cups sugar
1 cup sour cream
3 cups all-purpose flour

½ teaspoon baking soda
6 eggs
1 teaspoon vanilla extract

Preheat oven to 325 degrees. Cream butter and sugar together; add sour cream. Sift flour and baking soda together. Add to creamed mixture, alternately with eggs, one at a time, beating after each. Add vanilla. Pour into a greased and floured tube pan and bake for 1 hour 20 minutes.   *the lady*

CHEESECAKE

1 cup graham cracker crumbs	½ stick butter, melted
¼ cup sugar	

Preheat oven to 350 degrees. Mix ingredients together and pat onto bottom and sides of an 8-inch springform cake pan. Prepare filling.

Filling

2 eggs	1 cup sugar
12 ounces cream cheese, softened	½ teaspoon vanilla extract

Beat eggs and softened cream cheese together. Add sugar and vanilla. Beat until well blended. Pour into prepared crust. Bake for 25 to 30 minutes. Let cool for 10 minutes. Add topping.

Topping

½ cup sugar	½ teaspoon vanilla extract
1 cup sour cream	

Combine ingredients and put on top of cake; return to oven for 10 minutes.

Optional Fresh Fruit Topping

2 cups fresh raspberries, blueberries, strawberries, cherries, etc.	¾ cup water
	1 tablespoon butter
	2 tablespoons cornstarch
½ cup sugar	

In small saucepan, bring fruit, sugar, ½ cup water, and butter to a boil. Mix cornstarch and ¼ cup water together. Add to boiling pot, cooking and stirring constantly for 1 minute, or until thick. Cool to room temperature. Serve dollop on each slice of cheesecake, with a sprig of fresh mint for garnish. *Hint:* You can use a canned pie filling (blueberry, strawberry, or cherry) instead of fresh fruit.

the lady

CARAMEL APPLE CAKE WITH CARAMEL TOPPING

Cathy is McCall's mother. I think I know now where
McCall gets her knack for cooking.

2½ cups sugar	2 teaspoons vanilla extract
3 eggs	1 cup chopped walnuts
1½ cups vegetable oil	2½ cups diced apples,
3 cups all-purpose flour	canned or fresh

Preheat oven to 350 degrees. Cream together sugar, eggs, and oil. Add
flour; mix together until well blended. Add vanilla, nuts, and diced apples.
Spread into a lightly greased and floured 13×9-inch baking dish; bake for
45 to 60 minutes. Cake is done when toothpick inserted in center comes
out clean. When cake is done, punch holes in it with a knife and pour
topping over.

Caramel Topping

3 sticks butter	¼ cup milk
2 cups brown sugar	

Heat all ingredients together over medium heat. Bring to boil, stirring
constantly. Let boil for about 2 minutes. Pour over warm cake.

Cathy Holmes, Savannah, GA

CRÈME DE CACAO ANGEL CAKE

1 angel food cake, purchased or homemade (12 to 16 ounces)	2 tablespoons cocoa
¼ cup crème de cacao, more if desired	2 tablespoons confectioners sugar
1 cup heavy cream	2 tablespoons toasted sliced almonds or chopped nuts

Put cake bottom up on serving plate. With a cake test or fork, poke holes
in cake and slowly spoon on liqueur, letting it seep into cake. Whip cream,
cocoa, and confectioners sugar until soft peaks form; use to frost cake. Just
before serving, drizzle small amount of liqueur over frosting and sprinkle
with toasted almonds or chopped nuts. Pass more liqueur to serve with
cake. Makes 6 to 8 servings. *Diane Silver Berryhill, Savannah, GA*

MAMA'S QUICK FUDGE FROSTING

1 cup sugar	2 tablespoons corn syrup
¼ cup cocoa	⅛ teaspoon salt
½ stick butter	1½ to 2 cups powdered sugar
½ cup milk	1 teaspoon vanilla extract

Mix first six ingredients in saucepan; stir and bring to a full rolling boil.
Continue boiling, stirring occasionally, for 3 minutes. Syrup must become
thick and coat the spoon, so be sure mixture cooks at a hard rolling boil.
Remove from heat. Add powdered sugar and vanilla. Pour over warm pan
cake and brownies or frost round cakes. *the lady*

MAMA'S QUICKER FUDGE FROSTING

1 stick butter	1 box powdered sugar
3 tablespoons cocoa	1 teaspoon vanilla extract
⅓ cup milk	1 cup nuts, chopped

In a saucepan, combine butter, cocoa, and milk; bring to boil. Add sugar
and vanilla; beat well until smooth. Fold in nuts. Pour over warm cake.
the lady

CORRIE'S CARAMEL ICING

3¼ cups sugar	⅓ teaspoon baking soda
½ cup butter	1 cup milk

In a saucepan, caramelize ¼ cup of the sugar; add butter and set aside.
Combine baking soda and milk together and heat; add remaining sugar
and mix well. Pour into caramelized mixture. Heat to rolling boil for 8 to
10 minutes. Remove from heat and set in cold water; beat until creamy
and thick. *the lady*

POSIE CREAM ICING

A wonderful frosting for birthday cakes. Ideal for piping onto special-occasion cakes.

1   cup Crisco
¼   cup butter, softened
3   cups sifted 4X powdered sugar

⅛   teaspoon salt
1½ teaspoons vanilla extract

In a large bowl, at medium speed, mix shortening with butter. Beat in powdered sugar, salt, and vanilla until fluffy and smooth.   *the lady*

SEVEN-MINUTE ICING

2   egg whites
1½ cups sugar
1½ teaspoons white corn syrup

⅓   cup cold water
Dash of salt
1   teaspoon vanilla extract

Place all ingredients except vanilla in double boiler. Beat with mixer over boiling water until mixture stands in peaks, about 7 minutes. Add vanilla. Will frost tops and sides of two 9-inch layers.   *the lady*

CARAMEL ICING

2½ cups white sugar
½   cup water

1   cup milk
¾   stick butter

In a heavy saucepan, brown ½ cup of the sugar, add water, and stir until dissolved. Add milk to remaining white sugar and mix with brown sugar mixture. Cook together until this forms soft ball when tested in cold water. Do not stir while boiling. Add butter. This hardens quickly.   *the lady*

LEMON CHEESECAKE FILLING AND ICING

½ cup butter
1 cup sugar

6 egg yolks
Zest and juice of two lemons

Combine above ingredients in top of a double boiler; cook, stirring, until thick. Spread between layers of cake. Ice top and sides of cake.

Divinity Icing

2½ cups sugar
⅛ teaspoon salt
⅛ cup light corn syrup

⅔ cup water
2 egg whites
1 teaspoon vanilla extract

Dissolve sugar, salt, and syrup in water and heat. Beat egg whites until foamy. When syrup reaches boiling point, add 3 tablespoons to the egg whites and beat until stiff. Boil syrup until it spins a thread 10 inches long. Pour syrup over egg whites, beating constantly. Beat until it holds shape, add vanilla, and spread over cake. *Variation:* Before icing completely cools, sprinkle with coconut.   *Martha Ann Cutcliffe, Dunwoody, GA*

LEMON CHEESECAKE FILLING

1½ cups sugar
4 tablespoons cornstarch
4 tablespoons butter, melted
   Juice of 4 lemons

Zest of 1 lemon
6 egg yolks, slightly beaten
1 can applesauce

In a saucepan over medium heat, combine sugar and cornstarch; add butter, juice, and zest. Cook until mixture thickens. Stir small amount of hot mixture into egg yolks, then add egg mixture back into saucepan. Continue to cook another 1 to 2 minutes. Blend in applesauce.   *the lady*

WALNUT PRALINE BRIE WITH FRUIT

1 pound red or green grapes	2 teaspoons light corn syrup
¼ cup dark brown sugar	2 ounces chopped walnuts
4 teaspoons butter	1 small wheel of Brie (8 ounces)

Wash and divide grapes into clusters. Make praline: Place sugar, butter, corn syrup, and 1 teaspoon water in a small saucepan. Simmer for 3 minutes. Stir in walnuts. Cut Brie into wedges; arrange on round serving tray. Spoon 1 teaspoon praline mixture over each wedge. Garnish with grapes.

CRÈME CARAMEL

1 cup sugar	3 cups milk
5 eggs	1½ teaspoons vanilla extract
¼ teaspoon salt	

Preheat oven to 350 degrees. Butter eight 6-ounce custard cups. In a small skillet over medium heat, melt ½ cup sugar, stirring constantly until it is a light brown syrup. Pour syrup into buttered cups. Place cups in baking pan for easy handling. In large bowl with mixer at low speed, beat eggs, salt, and remaining ½ cup sugar until lemon-colored. Gradually beat in milk and vanilla. Once mixture has settled, with all air bubbles out, pour mixture into cups. Put hot water into baking pan to within 1 inch of top of cups. Bake 1 hour, or until knife inserted in center comes out clean. Cool, loosen custard with knife; invert. *Variation:* Sprinkle ground nutmeg on top of each custard before baking. *Kelley Ort, Atlanta, GA*

PEACH COBBLER

1	stick butter	1	28-ounce can sliced peaches
1	cup sugar		in syrup, undrained
¾	cup self-rising flour		(see Variation)
¾	cup milk		

Preheat oven to 350 degrees. Put butter in deep baking dish and place in oven to melt. Mix sugar and flour; add milk slowly to prevent lumping. Pour over melted butter. Do not stir. Spoon fruit on top, gently pouring in syrup. Still do not stir; batter will rise to top during baking. Bake for 30 to 45 minutes. Good with fresh whipped cream or vanilla ice cream.

Variation: When available, fresh fruit is wonderful. You may use fresh blueberries, strawberries, blackberries, cherries, apples, peaches, or pears. Simply clean, peel, and core 2 cups of fruit and mix with 1 cup of sugar and 1 cup of water. In a saucepan, bring mixture to a boil and then simmer for about 10 minutes. Stir often, making sure sugar is completely dissolved. Substitute this for the canned peaches. *the lady*

BANANA PUDDING

Mother would frequently have one of these warm wonderful puddings sitting on our kitchen counter waiting for Bubba and me to arrive home from school. What a special treat!

¾	cup sugar	1	teaspoon vanilla extract
3	tablespoons all-purpose flour	½	stick butter
2	cups milk	3	medium bananas, sliced
3	egg yolks		Vanilla wafers

Mix together sugar and flour and slowly add milk. This should be cooked in the top of a double boiler, but you can cook it over low to medium heat, stirring constantly until it thickens—do not leave it unattended. Slightly beat egg yolks and temper with a small amount of the hot custard; stir well. Add egg mixture to custard pot and cook 2 more minutes. Remove from heat and add vanilla and butter. Let cool. In a 13×9-inch casserole dish, alternate pudding, bananas, and wafers, beginning with pudding and ending with pudding. Add topping, if desired.

Meringue Topping

3	egg whites	6	tablespoons sugar
¼	teaspoon cream of tartar	1	teaspoon vanilla extract

Preheat oven to 350 degrees. Beat egg whites with cream of tartar and sugar until stiff. Add vanilla. Spread over pudding mix; completely seal around edge. Bake until desired brownness on top.

At the restaurant, I no longer prefer the meringue topping but instead like a fresh whipped topping. Of course, the pudding must be very cold before you add the whipped cream topping, otherwise the warmth from the pudding will break down the ingredients of the whipped cream. For fresh whipped cream: as you are beating 1 cup heavy cream, sweeten with ¼ cup sugar; add 1 teaspoon vanilla for extra flavor. —the lady

Even with this first cookbook, I was planning my next!

)COLATE ICE CREAM

y night our restaurant is open, I churn fresh ice cream myself for o..r guests. This chocolate seems to be a favorite, although we have many different flavors. We will have to save them for our next cookbook.

5 eggs
2½ to 3 cups sugar, depending
on how sweet you like.
I use 3 cups.
⅔ cup cocoa

1 can Eagle Brand
condensed milk
2 cups heavy cream
1 tablespoon vanilla extract
Whole milk

In electric mixer, beat eggs, sugar, and cocoa until well blended. Add canned milk, heavy cream, and vanilla and beat well. Pour into an electric ice cream churn. Add whole milk to bring mixture to fill line on ice cream churn. Churn until motor starts to labor. Remove blade; pack with additional ice and rock salt. Cover with towels and let stand for 1 to 2 hours.

LAYERED BLUEBERRY DESSERT

1 8-ounce package cream cheese
1 cup sugar
1 box Dream Whip, prepared

2 cups graham crackers crumbs
1 stick butter, melted
1 can blueberry pie filling

Cream together cream cheese and sugar; add prepared Dream Whip. Mix graham cracker crumbs and melted butter, and press one-half of crumbs in bottom of 13×9-inch dish. Add one layer of Dream Whip mixture, one layer of fruit filling, another layer of Dream Whip mixture, and sprinkle top with final layer of cracker crumbs.

BAKED CUSTARD

4 eggs	1 teaspoon vanilla extract
½ cup sugar	3 cups scalded milk
½ teaspoon salt	Ground nutmeg

Beat eggs slightly; add sugar, salt, and vanilla. Gradually add scalded milk, stirring constantly. Strain if desired. Sprinkle with nutmeg. Place in pan containing hot water. Water should cover ¾ of the way up the edge of custard dish. Bake at 375 degrees for about 30 minutes. *the lady*

SCHUBURGER MOUSSE

2 dozen macaroons, crumbled	½ teaspoon vanilla extract
½ cup bourbon or rum	½ cup chopped pecans
2 sticks butter	1 dozen double ladyfingers
1 cup sugar	¾ cup heavy cream, whipped
6 eggs, separated	with 3 tablespoons sugar
2 ounces unsweetened chocolate, melted	until stiff

Soak crumbled macaroons with bourbon or rum. Cream butter with sugar. Beat in lightly beaten egg yolks; add melted chocolate, vanilla, nuts, and macaroons. Beat egg whites until stiff; fold into chocolate mixture. Grease a springform pan; line with separated ladyfingers. Alternate layers of chocolate mixture with remaining ladyfingers. Chill overnight. Remove from pan and decorate with whipped cream. *Anne S. Hanson, Albany, GA*

GOURMET RICE PUDDING

1	cup short-grain white rice	½	stick butter
3	cups boiling water	½	cup raisins
½	teaspoon salt	1	tablespoon vanilla extract
1	14-ounce can sweetened condensed milk		

Measure rice, boiling water, and salt into top of double boiler. Cook over rapidly boiling water until rice is tender, about 40 minutes. Stir in condensed milk, butter, and raisins. Cook, stirring frequently, over boiling water until slightly thickened, about 20 minutes. Remove from heat and stir in vanilla. Serve warm or cold. Serves 8.   *Kelley Ort, Atlanta, GA*

BLUEBERRY PUDDING

1	21-ounce can blueberry pie mix	1	15-ounce box yellow cake mix
1	20-ounce can crushed pineapple, drained, juice reserved	1	cup chopped pecans
		1½	sticks butter

Put blueberry mix in bottom of 8×11-inch baking dish. Layer drained pineapple over blueberries, spread dry cake mix over top, and sprinkle nuts over all. Heat pineapple juice with butter and drizzle over mixture. Do not stir. Bake at 350 degrees for about 30 minutes.   *the lady*

HAWAIIAN PUDDING

1½ sticks butter, melted
¼ cup lemon juice
3 cups vanilla wafer crumbs
(one 11-ounce box)
3 bananas (sliced and placed
in the lemon juice)
2 20-ounce cans crushed
pineapple, drained

1 cup chopped nuts, divided
1 10-ounce can sweetened
condensed milk
1 8-ounce container Cool Whip
1 7-ounce bag coconut
1 10-ounce jar maraschino
cherries, drained

Mix together melted butter, lemon juice, and crumbs. Press in 13×9-inch dish or pan. Layer the bananas, pineapple, and half of the nuts. Pour condensed milk, spread Cool Whip, and sprinkle coconut and rest of nuts on top. Decorate with red cherries. Refrigerate overnight. Green cherries may be substituted for a wonderful St. Patrick's Day treat. Cool and refreshing; great light dessert for the summertime.

Diane Silver Berryhill, Savannah, GA

PEARS SABAYON

4 egg yolks
1 cup confectioners sugar
Dash of salt

¼ cup sherry
¾ cup heavy cream
1 29-ounce can pears, drained and chilled

Beat the egg yolks with sugar, salt, and wine in a saucepan or in top of a double boiler. Beat until smooth. Cook for 8 to 10 minutes, or until sauce thickens, stirring constantly. Remove from heat; let cool. Whip cream in a separate bowl until it holds peaks. When sauce is completely cooled, gently fold in whipped cream. Serve over chilled, drained pears. Quick and easy cool dessert—great during the holidays.

Diane Silver Berryhill, Savannah GA

LEMON LUSH

1	stick butter, at room temperature	1	cup all-purpose flour
		½	cup chopped nuts

Spray a 7×11-inch baking dish with nonstick cooking spray. Mix all ingredients and press into bottom of prepared dish. Bake at 350 degrees for about 20 minutes until slightly browned. Cool.

Filling #1

1	8-ounce package cream cheese, softened	1	cup frozen whipped topping, thawed
1	cup powdered sugar		

Mix together and spread over cooled crust.

Filling #2

2	3-ounce packages instant lemon pie filling	Zest and juice of 2 lemons
3	cups milk	Whipped topping, enough to cover
		Nuts (optional)

Mix pie filling with milk; beat 2 minutes. Add zest and lemon juice and mix well. Spread over filling #1. Top with whipped topping; sprinkle with nuts, if desired. Cut into squares for nice do-ahead dessert.

Susan Dupuy, Albany, GA

CHOCOLATE ALMOND PIE

16 to 20 large marshmallows		1	cup heavy cream
4	1½-ounce Hershey chocolate bars with almonds	1	teaspoon vanilla extract
½	cup milk	1	8-inch graham cracker crust

Melt marshmallows and candy bars in milk in double boiler. Remove from heat and cool. Whip cream until stiff and fold into cooled mixture. Add vanilla. Pour into prepared crust and chill. Good as is or top with whipped cream.

Virginia Robertson, Albany, GA

PASTRY FOR 2-CRUST PIE

For extra-tender pastry, cut in half of the shortening until the mixture is like cornmeal; then cut in the remaining shortening until it is like small peas.

2 cups sifted all-purpose flour	⅔ cup Crisco shortening
1 teaspoon salt	5 to 7 tablespoons cold water

Sift together flour and salt; cut in shortening with pastry blender until pieces are the size of small peas. Sprinkle 1 tablespoon water over part of mixture. Gently toss with fork; push to side of bowl. Repeat until all is moistened. Form into 2 balls. Flatten each on lightly floured surface by pressing with edge of hand three times across in both directions. Roll from center to edge until ⅛ inch thick.

the lady

FRENCH COCONUT PIE

½ stick butter	1 cup or 3½-ounce can
2 eggs, beaten	shredded coconut
1 tablespoon all-purpose flour	1 cup milk
¾ cup sugar	1 9-inch unbaked pie shell

Preheat oven to 400 degrees. Melt butter; add remaining ingredients. Pour into pie shell. Bake until firm, about 45 to 60 minutes.

Jacklyn Miller, Guyton, GA

154

BUTTERSCOTCH PIE

¾ cup brown sugar
5 tablespoons all-purpose flour
½ teaspoon salt
2 cups milk

2 egg yolks, lightly beaten
2 tablespoons butter
1 teaspoon vanilla extract
1 9-inch prebaked pie shell

Combine sugar, flour, and salt and stir in milk slowly. Cook in double boiler over boiling water until thickened, stirring constantly. Cover and cook 10 minutes longer, stirring occasionally. Add small amount of hot mixture to egg yolks, stirring rigorously. Add back to pot and cook 1 minute longer. Add butter and vanilla and cool. Place filling in pastry shell and cover with whipped cream or meringue.

Denise Watson, Albany, GA

CHOCOLATE DERBY PIE

Corrie is the daughter of my brother Bubba and Jill Hiers. She is my mother's namesake, and she is more like a granddaughter to me than a niece. I'll never forget the day she was born and her mother put her in my arms. The love I felt for her was immeasurable; I thought I had died and gone to heaven. Your "Auntie" loves ya' darling, just as much, if not more, today.

4 eggs, lightly beaten
2 cups sugar
1 12-ounce package semisweet chocolate chips, melted
1 cup sifted self-rising flour
2 sticks butter, melted

2 teaspoons vanilla extract
2 cups chopped pecans
2 9-inch unbaked deep-dish pie shells or 3 regular 9-inch unbaked pie shells

Preheat oven to 350 degrees. Combine eggs, sugar, and melted chocolate in large bowl. Add flour and mix well; stir in remaining ingredients except for pie shells. Spread mixture into pie shells. Bake for 30 minutes. Serve warm with ice cream. Freezes well! *Corrie W. Hiers, Albany, GA*

155

GRAPE PIE

4   cups Concord grapes, seeded
1   cup sugar
⅛   teaspoon salt

⅛   teaspoon ground cloves
1½ teaspoons tapioca
2   pie shells, unbaked

Slip skins from grapes and heat pulp; put through sieve to remove seeds. Combine pulp with skins and add remaining ingredients. Pour into 1 unbaked pie shell. Lightly roll 2nd pie pastry over top. Bake at 425 degrees for 30 to 40 minutes.   *Alberta DiClaudio, Savannah, GA*

FROZEN PEACH PIE FILLING

2   teaspoons Fruit-Fresh
3½ cups sugar
9   pounds fresh peaches, peeled, pitted, and sliced

1   teaspoon salt
½   cup plus 2 tablespoons quick-cooking tapioca
¼   cup lemon juice

Stir together Fruit-Fresh and sugar. Combine all ingredients with peaches. Line four pie pans with heavy foil or freezer paper. On top of foil, place plastic wrap. Let foil-and-plastic lining extend 5 inches all around each pan. Put 4 to 5 cups peach filling into each pan. Loosely cover filling with wraps and freeze until firm. Remove from pans, wrap tightly, and return to freezer until ready to use. When ready to use, just pop filling into pastry-lined pan, dot with butter, and sprinkle with ground nutmeg. Top with additional pastry. Bake at 425 degrees for about 1 hour.

Sheila Mims, Albany, GA

MAMA'S ANGEL PECAN PIE

3   egg whites
¼   teaspoon cream of tartar
1   cup sugar
1   teaspoon vanilla extract

1   cup chopped nuts
1   cup graham cracker crumbs
    Whipped topping

Beat egg whites until foamy and add cream of tartar; beat until stiff. Gradually add sugar. Add vanilla and chopped nuts. Fold in cracker crumbs. Pour into buttered pie plate. Bake at 325 degrees for 55 minutes. Cool and cover with whipped cream.

TOLL HOUSE PIE

2   eggs
½   cup all-purpose flour
½   cup packed brown sugar
½   cup granulated sugar
1   stick butter, melted

1   6-ounce package semisweet
    chocolate chips
1   cup chopped pecans or walnuts
1   9-inch unbaked pie shell
    Whipped topping (optional)

Preheat oven to 325 degrees. In large bowl, beat eggs until foamy. Add flour and brown sugar; beat until well blended. Blend in granulated sugar and butter. Stir in chocolate chips and nuts. Pour into pie shell. Bake for 1 hour. Cover with whipped topping, if desired.

Denise Watson, Albany, GA

COCONUT PIES (2)

4 eggs	1 teaspoon vanilla extract
1 stick butter, softened	1 7-ounce package coconut
2 cups sugar	2 unbaked pie shells
½ cup buttermilk	

In a mixing bowl, beat eggs; add butter and sugar. Blend until smooth. Add buttermilk and vanilla. Stir in coconut. Pour into pie shells. Bake at 350 degrees for 20 to 25 minutes, until brown.

the Lady

RITZ PECAN PIE

This is an old family recipe. It really is a pie—as it bakes, it makes its own crust.

3 egg whites	1½ cups chopped pecans
1 teaspoon baking powder	1 teaspoon vanilla extract
1½ cups sugar	2 cups heavy cream
20 Ritz Crackers, crumbled	

Preheat oven to 325 degrees. Grease a 9-inch pie pan. In a mixing bowl, beat egg whites with baking powder until stiff. Blend in 1 cup of the sugar, then add cracker crumbs, pecans, and vanilla. Pour into prepared pie pan and bake for 30 minutes. Meanwhile, in a medium bowl, whip cream with remaining ½ cup sugar until thick and spreadable. When pie is done, place on a rack to cool completely. Spread whipped cream over cooled pie.

the Lady

PECAN PIE

4 eggs	1½ cups pecans, chopped
¾ cup sugar	1 9-inch unbaked pie shell
1 cup dark corn syrup	Whipped cream, for serving
¼ cup butter, melted	

Beat eggs slightly; stir in sugar, corn syrup, and butter. Fold in nuts. Pour into pie shell and bake in center of oven at 350 degrees for 35 to 40 minutes, or until set. Serve topped with dollop of fresh whipped cream.

the Lady

INDIVIDUAL PECAN PIES

1   stick butter
1   cup all-purpose flour

1   3-ounce package
cream cheese

Preheat oven to 325 degrees. Soften cheese and butter and blend well. Stir in flour. Chill 1 hour. Shape into twenty-four 1-inch balls. Place in ungreased small muffin tins. Press down to form crust.

Filling

1   egg
¾   cup brown sugar
1   tablespoon butter

1   teaspoon vanilla extract
Dash of salt
⅔   cup chopped pecans

Beat egg, sugar, butter, vanilla, and salt until smooth. Divide half the nuts among pastry cups. Add egg mixture. Top with remaining nuts. Bake for 25 minutes, or until filling hardens.   *Virginia Robertson, Albany, GA*

PRALINE PUMPKIN PIE

⅓   cup finely chopped pecans
⅓   cup plus ½ cup brown sugar
2   tablespoons butter, softened
1   9-inch unbaked pie shell
3   whole eggs
2   eggs, separated
1   cup canned pumpkin
1½ cups heavy cream

¼   cup dark rum
½   teaspoon salt
1   teaspoon ground cinnamon
¼   teaspoon ground cloves
¼   teaspoon ground ginger
¼   teaspoon ground mace
    (optional)
2   tablespoons granulated sugar

Preheat oven to 400 degrees. Blend pecans with ⅓ cup brown sugar and softened butter. Press gently with the back of a spoon into bottom of pie shell. Blend all remaining ingredients except egg whites and granulated sugar. Pour into pie shell. Bake for about 50 minutes. Make a meringue by beating egg whites until stiff, adding the granulated sugar while beating. After pie has baked, remove from oven and cover with meringue. Return to 425-degree oven just to brown meringue.   *the Lady*

STRAWBERRY AND CREAM PIE

1 stick butter	2 eggs, beaten
1½ cups powdered sugar	1 8-inch graham cracker crust

Cream together butter and powdered sugar; add eggs. Beat ingredients until fluffy. Spread over crust. Chill. Add topping.

Topping

1½ cups sliced and sweetened strawberries, drained	1 cup whipped cream

Fold strawberries into whipped cream. Spread over chilled pie. Chill for at least 8 hours. Garnish with whole berries and mint leaves.

STRAWBERRY PARFAIT PIE

This recipe is cool and refreshing. If desired, substitute peach Jell-O and frozen peaches for a delightful peach parfait pie.

1 cup boiling water	1 9-inch prepared pie shell, or individual tart shells
1 3-ounce package strawberry Jell-O	
1 pint vanilla ice cream	1 pint heavy whipping cream, whipped
1 pound frozen strawberries, thawed and drained	

Combine boiling water and Jell-O. Fold in ice cream until smooth. Let stand until beginning to set. Fold in drained fruit; put into prepared shell(s) and garnish with whipped cream. This pie can be refrigerated but not frozen. *Barbara Tobin, Watertown, MA*

THANKSGIVING PIE

3	eggs	1	teaspoon vanilla extract
1	cup dark corn syrup	1	cup chopped pecans
½	cup sugar	1	9-inch unbaked pie shell
½	stick butter, melted		Whipped cream
1	cup canned pumpkin		

Preheat oven to 350 degrees. With hand beater, beat eggs well. Beat in corn syrup, sugar, butter, pumpkin, and vanilla until well blended. Arrange pecans in bottom of pie shell. Slowly pour egg mixture over them. Bake for 1 hour, or until knife inserted 1 inch from edge comes out clean. Serve with whipped cream.

CHERRY–CREAM CHEESE PIE

1	8-ounce package cream cheese, at room temperature	1	teaspoon vanilla extract
1	14-ounce can sweetened condensed milk	1	9-inch graham cracker crust
½	cup fresh lemon juice	1	21-ounce can cherry pie filling, chilled

In a mixing bowl, beat cream cheese until light and fluffy. Gradually add milk; stir until well blended. Stir in lemon juice and vanilla. Pour filling into crust and refrigerate for 2 to 3 hours. Top with pie filling before serving.

MAMA'S CHESS PIE

1 stick butter	¼ teaspoon salt
2 cups sifted cake flour	3 to 6 tablespoons ice water

Cut butter into dry ingredients. Slowly add ice water. Knead dough and roll out on dough board, or press into bottom and sides of a 9-inch pie plate.

Filling

2 sticks butter	1½ teaspoons vanilla extract
2 cups sugar	½ cup heavy cream
7 egg yolks, beaten	2 tablespoons cornmeal

Preheat oven to 350 degrees. Cream butter and sugar; add egg yolks, vanilla, and cream. Gently blend in cornmeal. Pour into chess pie pastry. Bake until light brown on top, about 35 to 45 minutes.

the lady

CHOCOLATE MARSHMALLOW PIE

16 large marshmallows	1 cup whipping cream
½ cup milk	1 9-inch pie shell,
1 8-ounce chocolate almond candy bar	baked

In top of a double boiler, combine marshmallows and milk. Place over boiling water; stir mixture until marshmallows are melted. Add chocolate bar; stir until melted and mixture is smooth. Cool to room temperature. Whip cream; fold into marshmallow mixture. Turn into baked pastry shell. Cover with waxed paper or clear plastic wrap. Refrigerate for at least 6 hours or overnight.

the lady

...ON PECAN PIE

cup butter, melted
1¼ cups sugar
3 eggs, beaten

1¼ cups pecans, finely chopped
Juice of 1 lemon
1 9-inch pie shell, unbaked

Mix all filling ingredients well. Bake in pie shell at 425 degrees for
5 minutes; reduce heat to 325 degrees and bake for 40 to 50 minutes,
until golden brown. Cool. *Audrey Murphy, Richmond Hill, GA*

MAGIC LEMON MERINGUE PIE

1 14-ounce can sweetened
condensed milk
½ cup lemon juice
1 teaspoon grated lemon zest

3 egg yolks
1 8-inch prebaked pie shell
or crumb crust

In medium bowl, combine milk, lemon juice, and zest; blend in egg yolks.
Pour into cooled crust.

Meringue

3 egg whites
¼ teaspoon cream of tartar

¼ cup sugar

Preheat oven to 325 degrees. Beat egg whites with cream of tartar until
soft peaks form. Gradually beat in sugar until stiff. Spread over filling;
seal to edge of crust. Bake for 12 to 15 minutes, or until meringue is
golden brown.

PUMPKIN PIE

1½ cups canned pumpkin	¼ teaspoon ground cloves
¾ cup sugar	2 slightly beaten eggs
½ teaspoon salt	1⅔ cups evaporated milk
1 teaspoon ground cinnamon	1 9-inch unbaked pie shell
¼ teaspoon ground ginger	Whipped cream, for serving

Combine pumpkin, sugar, salt, cinnamon, ginger, and cloves; blend in eggs. Stir in evaporated milk. Pour into pastry shell. Bake at 425 degrees for 15 minutes. Reduce oven temperature to 350 degrees and bake for 45 minutes, or until knife inserted just off-center comes out clean. Remove from heat, cool, and serve with fresh whipped cream.

BANANA CREAM PIE

⅓ cup plus ¼ cup sugar	2 tablespoons butter
3 tablespoons cornstarch	2 teaspoons vanilla extract
¼ teaspoon salt	2 egg whites
1½ cups milk	2 bananas, sliced
2 egg yolks, lightly beaten	1 9-inch prebaked pie shell

In a saucepan over medium heat, combine ⅓ cup sugar with the cornstarch and salt. Blend in milk, then egg yolks. Cook and stir until mixture thickens. Remove from heat; stir in butter and vanilla. Cool to room temperature. Beat egg whites until soft peaks form; gradually add ¼ cup sugar and beat until stiff peaks form. Fold into egg yolk mixture. In pie shell, alternate layers of banana slices and cream filling. Cover and chill. Top with whipped cream and additional sliced bananas, if desired.

Candies & Cookies

Peggy, do you think we can make the next gingerbread man 6'2 with eyes of blue?

BREAKFAST COOKIES

Everyone will love these great cookies—
grab a handful as you go out the door.

⅔ cup butter, softened
⅔ cup sugar
1 egg
1 teaspoon vanilla extract
¾ cup all-purpose flour
½ teaspoon baking soda
½ teaspoon salt

1½ cups uncooked Quaker oats
1 cup Cheddar cheese, shredded
½ cup wheat germ, or finely
  chopped nuts
6 crisp cooked bacon slices,
  crumbled

Beat together butter, sugar, egg, and vanilla until well blended. Add the combined flour, baking soda, and salt; mix well. Stir in oats, cheese, wheat germ, and bacon. Drop by rounded tablespoonfuls onto greased cookie sheet. Bake at 350 degrees for 12 to 14 minutes, or until edges are golden brown. Cool 1 minute on cookie sheet, remove to wire cooling rack. Makes about 2 dozen cookies.

Diane Silver Berryhill, Savannah, GA

✔ *From one of my Savannah friends who contributed several wonderful recipes.*

CHOW MEIN NOODLE CANDY

1 6-ounce package semisweet
  chocolate morsels
1 6-ounce package butterscotch
  morsels

1 5-ounce can chow mein
  noodles
1 cup nuts, finely chopped

Combine chips in heavy pan and melt over lowest heat. When melted, add noodles and nuts. Mix well and drop by spoonfuls onto waxed paper. Cool and enjoy.

Diane Silver Berryhill, Savannah, GA

166

TEA COOKIES

2   sticks butter, softened
½   cup buttermilk
2   eggs
2   cups sugar
2½   cups all-purpose flour
1   tablespoon vanilla extract
1   teaspoon baking soda
1   teaspoon salt

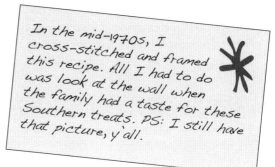

In the mid-1970s, I cross-stitched and framed this recipe. All I had to do was look at the wall when the family had a taste for these Southern treats. PS: I still have that picture, y'all.

Mix thoroughly. Bake at 350 degrees and check after 10 minutes.

Glennis Hiers, Statesboro, GA

LADY LOCK COOKIES

4   sticks butter
4   cups all-purpose flour
1   teaspoon salt

1   cup sour cream
1   cup buttermilk

Cut butter into dry ingredients. Add sour cream and buttermilk. Mix well. Divide into four parts, flour well, and fold like a rectangular envelope. Refrigerate overnight. Preheat oven to 375 degrees. Remove one part at a time, and roll thin. Make strips 1 inch wide and 7 inches long. Wrap around foil-covered clothespins. Bake for 15 minutes, or longer if needed. Set aside to cool.

Filling

1½   cups Crisco shortening
1   stick butter
1   cup sugar

1   egg white
2   teaspoons vanilla extract
½   cup hot milk

Cream together shortening and butter. Add sugar and beat well. Add egg white and vanilla; beat thoroughly. Add hot milk, 1 tablespoon at a time, and beat until creamy. Put into cookie press or pastry tube and fill cookies.

Janet DiClaudio, Savannah, GA

OLD-FASHIONED TEA CAKES

Frances is another close friend of my Aunt Peggy. Frances,
Peggy Richardson, and Aunt Peggy enjoy taking trips together.
Thanks for sharing your recipes with us.

4	cups all-purpose flour	2	eggs
1	teaspoon baking soda	½	cup buttermilk
2	teaspoons baking powder	2	sticks butter, softened
2	cups sugar	1	teaspoon vanilla extract

Preheat oven to 350 degrees. In a large bowl, sift flour, baking soda, and
baking powder together. Add remaining ingredients and blend well. Dough
should be soft. Roll dough out onto a floured surface until approximately
¼ inch thick. Cut dough into desired shapes and bake on a slightly greased
sheet for 10 to 12 minutes. *Frances Finney, Albany, GA*

GRANDMA'S GERMAN COOKIES

¼	cup sugar	½	teaspoon baking soda
1	stick butter	1	teaspoon cream of tartar
1	egg		Pinch of salt
1	cup all-purpose flour		

Preheat oven to 350 degrees. Cream together sugar, butter, and egg.
Sift dry ingredients together; add to egg mixture. Pour into greased
13×9×2-inch baking pan. Bake for 10 to 12 minutes. Cool. Prepare icing.

Icing

1	cup powdered sugar	½	teaspoon vanilla extract
½	stick butter		Small amount of milk

Combine sugar and butter; add vanilla. Add just enough milk
for desired consistency. Pour onto
cooled baked batter. Cut into squares.
Jody Moyer, Muncie, IN

Jody is one
of my Yankee
friends who
landed in Albany,
Georgia.

CHEESE COOKIES

½	pound sharp cheese, grated		Dash of salt
2	sticks butter, softened	½	teaspoon Worcestershire sauce
2	cups flour		(optional)
½	teaspoon cayenne pepper	2	cups Rice Krispies

Using a mixer, combine cheese and butter. Combine flour, pepper, and salt; slowly add to cheese mixture until well blended. Add Worcestershire sauce (if desired) and Rice Krispies; mix well. Form into small balls; place on ungreased cookie sheet. Press flat with floured fork. Bake at 375 degrees for 7 minutes. Should be slightly brown.

LADY BROWNIES

2	cups sugar	1	teaspoon vanilla extract
1	cup vegetable oil	1½	cups self-rising flour
4	eggs	1	cup chopped walnuts
6	tablespoons cocoa		or pecans

Preheat oven to 325 degrees. Blend together sugar, oil, eggs, cocoa, and vanilla. Add flour; mix. Add nuts; spread into greased 13×9-inch baking dish. Bake for 25 to 30 minutes.

CREAM CHEESE BROWNIES

Use Lady Brownies recipe above. Pour half the batter into a greased pan. Layer with this cream cheese mixture, then top with remaining batter, swirling it with a knife.

1	stick butter, softened	2	eggs
1	8-ounce package cream cheese,	1	tablespoon all-purpose flour
	softened	1	cup chopped walnuts
½	cup sugar		or pecans

Cream together butter and cream cheese. Add remaining ingredients; blend well. Swirl into brownie batter with knife edge.

SLICED NUT COOKIES

1 cup granulated sugar	1 teaspoon baking powder
1 cup brown sugar	1 teaspoon salt
1½ cups Crisco shortening	1 teaspoon ground cinnamon
3 eggs, beaten	1 teaspoon ground nutmeg
4½ cups all-purpose flour	½ teaspoon ground cloves
1 teaspoon baking soda	1 cup ground pecans

Cream sugars and shortening; add eggs. Sift together flour, baking soda, baking powder, and salt; add to sugar mixture. Add cinnamon, nutmeg, cloves, and nuts. Roll into several small, oblong rolls. Chill until cold. Preheat oven to 375 degrees. Slice dough into thin cookies. Bake for 12 minutes.

Denise Watson, Albany, GA

NEVER-FAIL PEANUT BRITTLE

3 cups white sugar	3 teaspoons butter
1 cup white corn syrup	1 teaspoon salt
½ cup water	2 teaspoons baking soda
3 cups raw peanuts	

Boil sugar, syrup, and water until thread spins, then add peanuts. Stir often. Cook until temperature reaches 280 degrees, or until hard when tested in cold water. Take from stove; add butter, salt, and baking soda. (Sift baking soda so that there will be no lumps.) Pour onto buttered pan or large cookie sheet to cool.
Break into small pieces.

Virginia Robertson, Albany, GA

We called Corrie's grandmother "Mrs. Rob," and Corrie's heart is full of so many fond memories of her.

CHOCOLATE ÉCLAIRS

Pastry

1 cup plus 1 tablespoon water	1 cup sifted all-purpose flour
1 stick butter	5 eggs

Filling

3 cups rich milk	6 tablespoons all-purpose flour
¾ cup sugar	3 eggs, slightly beaten
½ teaspoon salt	2 teaspoons vanilla extract

Icing

2 1-ounce squares unsweetened chocolate	2 cups sugar
	1 cup whipping cream

Heat 1 cup of the water and butter to boiling point. Add flour and stir constantly until dough pulls away from sides of pan and is smooth and shiny. Remove from heat and let cool. Beat in 4 of the eggs, one at a time. Drop dough from teaspoon onto greased cookie sheet to form small éclairs. In a small bowl, whisk together remaining egg and 1 tablespoon of the water. Brush tops of éclairs with egg wash. Bake at 375 degrees for approximately 30 minutes, or until light brown. Set aside to cool. Prepare filling by combining milk, sugar, salt, and flour; cook slowly until thickens. Add 3 beaten eggs and continue to cook until mixture is even thicker. Remove from heat, cool, and add vanilla. Cut off tops of pastry puffs and fill with the custard mixture; replace tops. Melt chocolate for icing; add sugar and cream. Cook over medium heat until soft-ball stage. Let cool and beat until smooth. Ice tops of the éclairs. Makes approximately 12 large, 24 medium, or 60 small éclairs.   *Jill Hiers, Albany, GA*

MAMA'S TEA CAKES

2 sticks butter, softened	4 cups all-purpose flour
1¾ cups sugar	1 teaspoon baking powder
2 large eggs	1 teaspoon baking soda
1 tablespoon vanilla extract	

Cream together butter and sugar; add eggs and vanilla. Sift together the flour, baking powder, and baking soda; combine with egg mixture. Bake at 325 degrees for 12 minutes, or until golden brown.

Carolyn Cundiff, Athens, GA

UNBAKED COOKIES

½ cup cocoa	3 cups quick oatmeal
½ cup butter	2 tablespoons peanut butter
½ cup milk	1 tablespoon vanilla extract
2 cups sugar	

Combine first four ingredients in saucepan over medium heat. Bring to a boil and let boil for 1½ minutes. Remove from heat, but while mixture is still hot, stir in oatmeal, peanut butter, and vanilla. Drop on waxed paper (1 heaping teaspoon per cookie) and let cool.

Alberta DiClaudio, Savannah, GA

GOODIES

2 sticks butter	1 teaspoon vanilla extract
2 cups packed brown sugar	⅓ cup peanut butter
1 cup light corn syrup	1½ cups uncooked rolled oats
½ teaspoon salt	½ cup chopped pecans
1 teaspoon vinegar	

Melt butter in large saucepan. Stir in brown sugar, syrup, salt, and vinegar. Cook over high heat to firm-ball stage. Remove from heat. Stir in remaining ingredients; pour into greased 8-inch square pan and chill. Cut into squares. Wrap each piece in wax paper.

Virginia Robertson, Albany, GA

THUMBPRINT COOKIES

3 sticks butter, softened	¼ teaspoon salt
1 cup sugar	1 teaspoon vanilla extract
2 egg yolks	Any tart preserves
3¾ cups all-purpose flour	(plum, for example)

Cream butter and sugar. Add egg yolks. Sift flour and salt; blend into butter mixture. Add vanilla. Chill dough thoroughly. Preheat oven to 350 degrees. Shape dough into 1-inch balls and place on an ungreased cookie sheet. Make indentation in center of each with thumb; fill with preserves (jelly or pecan halves will also work). Bake for 15 minutes, or until lightly browned. Cool slightly; remove to rack to finish cooling. These keep well in a tightly closed container.   *Jill Hiers, Albany, GA*

PEANUT BUTTER BUCKEYES

1 12-ounce jar crunchy peanut butter (1½ cups)	2 sticks butter
1 16-ounce box powdered sugar	1 12-ounce package semisweet chocolate chips
	1 bar paraffin

Mix together peanut butter, sugar, and butter and form into small balls; chill. Over medium heat in the top of a double boiler, melt together the chocolate and paraffin. Using a toothpick, dip each ball into chocolate and cover about three-quarters of the ball, leaving a brown round eye. Place on wax paper to cool.   *the Lady*

CHOCOLATE FUDGE

3 cups sugar	1 cup milk
4 heaping tablespoons cocoa	¾ stick butter
3 tablespoons white corn syrup	1½ teaspoons vanilla extract

Mix sugar and cocoa; add syrup and milk. Cook until temperature on a candy thermometer reaches 244 degrees, firm-ball stage. Add butter and vanilla. Beat with mixer. Pour into slightly buttered dish and cut into squares.   *the Lady*

BERNICE'S CHEWY COOKIES

1 stick butter	2 cups all-purpose flour
1 16-ounce box brown sugar	1½ teaspoons baking powder
4 eggs, lightly beaten	Pinch of salt
½ teaspoon vanilla extract	2 cups chopped pecans

Preheat oven to 300 degrees. Melt butter and sugar together in the top of a double boiler; remove from heat. Add eggs and vanilla. In a bowl, combine flour, baking powder, and salt. Add to egg mixture; mix well. Stir in nuts. Drop spoonfuls onto greased cookie sheet and bake for 15 to 20 minutes.

Carolyn Cundiff, Athens, GA

SNICKERDOODLES

1 cup Crisco shortening	2 teaspoons cream of tartar
1½ cups plus 2 tablespoons sugar	1 teaspoon baking soda
2 eggs	½ teaspoon salt
2¾ cups sifted all-purpose flour	2 teaspoons ground cinnamon

Preheat oven to 350 degrees. Cream shortening, 1½ cups sugar, and eggs. Sift together flour, cream of tartar, baking soda, and salt. Combine with egg mixture. Chill dough thoroughly and then roll into balls the size of a small walnut. Roll in mixture of 2 tablespoons sugar and the cinnamon. Bake for 8 to 10 minutes on an ungreased baking sheet until lightly browned but still soft.

Denise Watson, Albany, GA

MACAROONS

3 egg whites	½ cup granulated sugar
1 teaspoon vanilla extract	½ cup light brown sugar
1 teaspoon distilled white vinegar	1 cup nuts, finely ground

Beat egg whites to soft peaks; add vanilla and vinegar. Add granulated sugar, 1 teaspoon at a time; fold in brown sugar and nuts. Drop onto wax-paper-lined cookie sheets. Bake at 200 degrees for 1 hour.

Claudine Arnsdorff, Springfield, GA

ROME COOKIES

1 16-ounce box graham crackers	½ cup milk
1½ sticks butter	1 cup chopped pecans
1 cup sugar	1 cup or 3½-ounce can
1 egg	shredded coconut

Line a 13×9-inch pan with whole graham crackers. Melt butter in saucepan and add sugar. Beat egg and milk together; add to butter mixture. Bring to a boil, stirring constantly. Remove from heat. Add nuts, coconut, and 1 cup graham cracker crumbs. Pour over crackers in pan. Cover with another layer of whole graham crackers. Prepare topping.

Topping

2 cups powdered sugar	½ stick butter
1 teaspoon vanilla extract	3 tablespoons milk

Beat all ingredients together and spread over top layer of crackers. Chill. Cut into squares.   *Janet DiClaudio, Savannah, GA*

MAMA'S BOURBON BALLS
I remember Mama serving these every Christmas.
The adults always enjoyed them immensely,
and my brother Bubba and I enjoyed sneaking one.

2½ cups crushed vanilla wafers	1 cup chopped pecans
2 tablespoons cocoa	3 tablespoons light corn syrup
1 cup powdered sugar	¼ cup bourbon

Mix ingredients together and form into small balls. Makes about 40 to 45 balls. Roll in additional powdered sugar, if desired.

CHOCOLATE POPCORN

½ cup sugar	2 tablespoons cocoa
½ cup light corn syrup	½ teaspoon salt
½ stick butter	8 cups popped corn

Over medium heat, in a 4-quart pot, bring sugar, corn syrup, butter, cocoa, and salt to a boil. Stir in popped corn. Cook and stir until popcorn is coated, about 2 minutes. Cool to lukewarm. Shape into 3-inch balls.

CHOCOLATE BALLS

2 boxes 4X powdered sugar	1 teaspoon almond flavoring
1 stick butter, softened	1 large package coconut
1 can condensed milk	1½ cups chopped nuts

Cream together sugar and butter; add milk. Stir in almond flavoring, coconut, and nuts; mix well. Form into 1-inch balls. Place on waxed paper and refrigerate for at least 3 hours.

Coating

1 bar paraffin	1 package semisweet chocolate chips

In top of a double boiler, melt paraffin and chocolate, stirring constantly. With a toothpick, dip each ball in chocolate coating and place on wax paper until set.

CHOCOLATE FUDGE

4½ cups sugar	12 ounces German sweet
⅓ teaspoon salt	chocolate, broken
2 tablespoons butter	1 pint marshmallow creme
1 12-ounce can evaporated milk	2 cups chopped nuts
12 ounces chocolate chips	

In a saucepan, bring first four ingredients to a boil. Cook for 7 minutes. Pour over chocolate. Stir until chocolate is melted. Add marshmallow and nuts. Pour into lightly buttered pan.

FIVE-MINUTE FUDGE

1⅔ cups sugar	1 6-ounce bag semisweet chocolate chips
⅔ cup evaporated milk	16 large marshmallows
1 tablespoon butter	1 teaspoon vanilla extract
½ teaspoon salt	1 cup chopped pecans

Combine sugar, milk, butter, and salt in a saucepan. Bring to a boil and cook for 5 minutes, stirring constantly. Add chocolate chips and continue to heat until chocolate is melted. Remove from heat and stir in marshmallows, vanilla, and nuts; mix well. Pour into shallow 8-inch square pan to cool; cut into squares.   *the lady*

QUICK 'N' EASY OATMEAL COOKIES

1 cup boiling water	1 cup chopped nuts
1 cup raisins	1½ teaspoons baking soda
1 cup shortening	1 teaspoon salt
1 cup sugar	1 teaspoon ground cinnamon
2 eggs	1 teaspoon vanilla extract
2 cups Pillsbury blending flour	½ teaspoon ground nutmeg
2 cups quick-cooking rolled oats	¼ teaspoon ground cloves

Preheat oven to 375 degrees. Pour water over raisins and shortening. Add remaining ingredients; mix thoroughly. Drop by rounded teaspoonfuls onto greased cookie sheets. Bake for 10 to 12 minutes, or until light brown.   *the lady*

BUTTER FINGERS

1 cup chopped pecans	2 sticks butter
2½ cups all-purpose flour	1 teaspoon vanilla extract
¾ cup granulated sugar	1 16-ounce box powdered sugar

Preheat oven to 325 degrees. Combine all ingredients except for powdered sugar. Roll into small "fingers" or balls. Bake for 20 to 30 minutes. Roll immediately in powdered sugar. Makes approximately 100 cookies.   *the lady*

PECAN CLUSTERS

1	7-ounce jar marshmallow fluff	1	12-ounce can evaporated milk
1½	pounds chocolate kisses	1	stick butter
5	cups sugar	6	cups pecan halves

Place marshmallow fluff and kisses into a large bowl. Set aside. Combine sugar, milk, and butter in a saucepan. Bring to a boil and cook for 8 minutes. Pour over marshmallow and chocolate, stirring until well blended. Stir in pecans. Drop by teaspoonfuls onto wax paper. Makes about 12 dozen. *the lady*

M&M CANDY COOKIES

1	cup shortening	2¼	cups sifted all-purpose flour
1	cup brown sugar	1	teaspoon baking soda
½	cup granulated sugar	1	teaspoon salt
2	eggs	1½	cups M&M's plain candies
2	teaspoons vanilla extract		

Blend shortening and both sugars. Beat in eggs, one at a time; add vanilla. Sift flour, soda, and salt together and add to mixture; mix well. Stir in ½ cup of the M&M's. Drop by spoonfuls onto ungreased cookie sheet; decorate with remaining M&M's. Bake at 375 degrees for 10 to 12 minutes. *the lady*

PEANUT BUTTER BARS

1	stick butter	2	eggs
½	cup peanut butter	1	teaspoon vanilla extract
1½	cups sugar	1	cup self-rising flour

Preheat oven to 350 degrees. Grease and flour a 13×9×2-inch pan. Melt butter and peanut butter in bowl over hot water. Add remaining ingredients. Stir until blended. Pour into prepared pan and bake for 25 to 30 minutes. Cool and cut into squares. *Suzette Dupuy, Albany, GA*

PEANUT BUTTER BALLS

My grandparents owned the River Bend Motel and Restaurant,
which my Grandfather Paul built. As a small child, I attended a very
small country school situated just on the county line in Baconton.
Lunch on Fridays always consisted of soup, toasted bread, and
peanut butter balls. I would literally fight anyone for my share of
these treats. It was then, and still is, a wonderful snack for children.

1   cup peanut butter
1   cup honey
2   cups powdered milk

1½ cups crushed cornflakes, 1½
     cups finely chopped nuts of your
     choice, or 1 cup powdered sugar
1   cup melted chocolate (optional)

Mix peanut butter, honey, and milk together to form very thick mixture.
Roll out in small balls about the size of a walnut. Then roll in crushed
cornflakes, finely chopped nuts, or powdered sugar. Place on wax paper
and refrigerate. Roll balls in melted chocolate before coating, if desired.

Baconton Elementary School, Baconton, GA

CHOCOLATE BUTTERSCOTCH SQUARES

2   sticks butter
16   ounces dark brown sugar
4   eggs, beaten
½   cup plus 1 tablespoon flour
1   teaspoon baking powder
1   teaspoon salt

2   teaspoons vanilla extract
1   12-ounce package
     semisweet chocolate chips
1   cup pecans, chopped
     Whipped cream (optional)

Preheat oven to 350 degrees. In a saucepan over low heat, melt butter;
add brown sugar. Cook, stirring frequently, until sugar melts; remove from
heat; cool. Add eggs; mix well. Combine flour, baking powder, and salt;
add to egg mixture. Mix well. Fold in vanilla, chocolate chips, and nuts.
Grease a 13×9-inch baking pan. Pour in batter. Bake at 350 degrees for
40 to 45 minutes. Cut into squares. Serve warm with whipped cream.

the Lady

179

FUDGIE SCOTCH RING

1 6-ounce package semisweet chocolate chips	1 14-ounce can sweetened condensed milk
1 6-ounce package butterscotch morsels	1 cup coarsely chopped walnuts, plus 1 cup walnut halves
	½ teaspoon vanilla extract

In top of double boiler, melt chocolate and butterscotch together with milk. Stir occasionally until mixture begins to thicken. Remove from heat; add chopped walnuts and vanilla. Blend well. Chill for 1 hour until mixture thickens. Line bottom of a 9-inch pan with a 12-inch square of foil. Place ¾ cup walnut halves in bottom of pan, forming a 2-inch-wide flat ring. Spoon chocolate mixture in small mounds on top of walnuts to form a ring. Garnish with remaining walnut halves. Chill until firm enough to slice. Makes about 36 slices.

the Lady

NO-BAKE SQUARES

1 cup light corn syrup	12 ounces chunky peanut butter
1 cup granulated sugar	4½ cups Special K cereal
¼ teaspoon salt	

In a saucepan, bring first three ingredients just to a boil. Remove from heat and stir in peanut butter. Beat until smooth. Gently stir in cereal (don't stir too much). Butter a 13×9-inch cookie sheet. Spread mixture on, put a little butter on hands, and pat out thin. Cover with icing.

Icing

1 6-ounce package semisweet chocolate chips	1 6-ounce package butterscotch chips

Using a double boiler over hot water, melt chocolate and butterscotch. Spread over the cookie mixture quickly to give an attractive glaze. Cut into squares or bars.   *Elizabeth Denny Adams (Mrs. John L.), Savannah, GA*

CHOCOLATE DAMNATION

1 19.8-ounce package brownie mix	2 eggs, separated
12 ounces semisweet chocolate	¼ cup coffee liqueur
¼ cup strong black brewed coffee	3 tablespoons sugar
	¼ cup heavy cream

Prepare brownie batter according to directions on box. Pour into a greased 13×9×2-inch pan. Bake according to instructions on box. When cool, cut into squares and remove from pan. Clean pan thoroughly and grease once more. Place brownies back in greased pan. Combine chocolate and coffee in top of double boiler, and melt over boiling water. Remove from heat. Beat egg yolks and stir in small amount of chocolate mixture; pour mixture into balance of chocolate mixture; stir until smooth. Stir in liqueur and set aside to cool. Beat egg whites until foamy; gradually add sugar and beat until stiff. Whip cream until stiff. Fold cream into chocolate mixture; fold in egg whites. Pour filling over brownies. Cover with plastic wrap and chill 3 to 4 hours, until firm. Invert onto serving platter and drizzle on glaze. Let set and decorate with chocolate curls, if desired.

Chocolate Glaze

4 ounces semisweet chocolate	3 tablespoons strong black brewed coffee

Combine chocolate and coffee in double boiler. Heat until melted. Stir well.   *Shelly Peay, Richmond Hill, GA*

BUSY-DAY BROWNIES

¾ cup sifted self-rising flour	5 tablespoons cocoa
½ cup shortening	1 teaspoon vanilla extract
1 cup sugar	½ cup walnuts or pecans, chopped
2 eggs	

Mix all ingredients together; beat 3 minutes, until just blended. Pour into greased 9-inch square pan. Bake at 325 degrees for 30 minutes. For chewy brownies, bake for 20 to 25 minutes.   *the lady*

GRANDMOTHER PAUL'S CARAMEL POPCORN

1	cup butter	½	cup dark corn syrup
2	cups packed brown sugar	1	teaspoon baking soda
1	teaspoon salt	8	quarts popped popcorn

Over medium heat, combine first four ingredients and boil for 5 minutes. Remove from heat; stir in baking soda. Stir well. Pour over popcorn. Stir to coat well. Bake in large roaster or pan at 200 degrees for 1 hour, stirring every 15 minutes. Spread on waxed paper to dry.

Aunt Trina Bearden, Houma, LA

MAY-MAY'S BUTTER COOKIES

Karen is a fine artist, and we have the pleasure of displaying her art in our restaurant.

1	cup sugar, plus more for dipping	2	egg yolks
		1	tablespoon vanilla extract
3	sticks butter	3	cups bread flour

Gradually cream 1 cup of the sugar into butter. Add egg yolks and vanilla. Mix well. Add flour, gradually. Decide whether you want to use the dough in a cookie press, roll it out and use cookie cutters, or slice cookies. Shape the dough accordingly. Refrigerate for 2 hours, or until ready to bake. Preheat oven to 375 degrees. Form dough into cookies, using whatever method you chose, and place on an ungreased cookie sheet. Bake for 10 to 15 minutes. Do not let them get brown. Use spatula to remove and place on rack to cool. When cool, dip in remaining sugar.

May-May was my grandmother. We would bake these cookies together at Christmas time. She used a cookie press, which I always found difficult to manage since the dough has to be exactly the right temperature. She used to decorate the cookies making chocolate collars with little silver balls for the dogs and using colored frosting to make decorations for the little Christmas trees. She would roll crescents between her hands and make little balls of dough which we would press a thimble into to make a little "well" to fill with strawberry jam. Her cookies were truly magical.

Karen Nangle, Savannah, GA

Chefs d' Jour

the
Cook

a pinch of this...
a pinch of that...
and let the good times
roll —

BOBBY'S PIMENTO CHEESE

This is my son Bobby's own recipe for pimento cheese. Whenever we have pimento cheese sandwiches at our home, everyone wants Bobby to make them because this recipe is a definite favorite.

These three recipes are from three men I have loved since the day they were born.

1 3-ounce package cream cheese, softened
1 cup grated sharp Cheddar cheese
1 cup grated Monterey Jack cheese
½ cup mayonnaise
½ teaspoon House Seasoning
2 to 3 tablespoons mashed pimentos
1 teaspoon grated onion (optional)
  Cracked black pepper to taste

With an electric mixer, beat cream cheese until fluffy. Add remaining ingredients and beat until well blended.

Bobby Deen, The Lady & Sons Restaurant

BUBBA'S BEER BISCUITS

My brother, Bubba, confines most of his cooking to his charcoal grill, but he does come into the kitchen quite often to bake up these great biscuits. Love ya lots, Bubba—Your Sister.

4 cups Bisquick
¼ to ½ cup sugar

1 12-ounce can of beer
2 tablespoons butter, melted

Preheat oven to 400 degrees. Mix all ingredients well, adjusting the sugar according to how sweet a biscuit you prefer. Pour into well-greased muffin tins. Bake for 15 to 20 minutes. Serve with honey butter.

Bubba Hiers, Albany, GA

JAMIE'S CHICKEN SALAD

My son Jamie has perfected this recipe and enjoys altering it to accommodate different occasions. He does a wonderful job in the kitchen as well as looking after the business management of the restaurant.

1	2½- to 3-pound chicken	½	cup mayonnaise
	Salt and pepper to taste	1	teaspoon lemon-pepper
1	onion, quartered		seasoning
2	ribs plus 1 cup chopped celery	¼	teaspoon pepper
4	hard-boiled eggs, chopped		2 to 3 tablespoons chicken
2	teaspoons Jane's Krazy Mixed-Up Salt		stock

Put the chicken in a large stockpot along with salt, pepper, onion, and celery stalks. Boil chicken until well done. Reserve stock. Remove chicken from pot. Cool; remove skin and bones. Dice the chicken and combine it with chopped celery and eggs in a large bowl. Add remaining ingredients and mix well. Serves 6 to 8.   *Jamie Deen, The Lady & Sons Restaurant*

I am so proud of my sons for the manner in which they conduct themselves in the day-to-day operation of our restaurant. Their eagerness and willingness to accept responsibilities and carry extra workloads to make our business a success is without measure. They have matured into fine, wonderful men that would make any mother proud. My sons are truly the wind beneath my wings. They are my heroes.

CANDIED DILLS

Paul is a high school colleague who now resides in Washington, DC.
He left Georgia for a Congress-related career, but kept his South
Georgia roots by working with two members of Congress who represented
Savannah in the House of Representatives. Thanks for your contribution
to our book and our political interests, Paul.

1 quart whole dill pickles	½ cup tarragon vinegar
2¾ cups sugar	2 tablespoons pickling spice

Drain pickles, cut into ½-inch slices, and place in a deep glass or ceramic
bowl. Add sugar and vinegar. Place pickling spice in a small square of
cheesecloth, tie closed, and add to bowl. Let stand at room temperature
until sugar is dissolved, about 4 hours. Pour pickles into a 1-quart jar,
cover, and refrigerate. Pickles taste best after 2 or 3 days. Remove spice
bag after one week.   *Paul Powell, Washington, DC*

DADDY'S BARBECUE SAUCE

I have so many fond memories of my cheerleading team coming to our
house. Daddy would barbecue chicken for us in the backyard. My daddy
was well loved by all who knew him. Thanks, Bubba, for submitting this
recipe. The cookbook would be incomplete without it.

1 cup Worcestershire sauce	Juice of 2 lemons
½ stick butter	

Mix ingredients together and simmer for 10 minutes. For good charcoal
grilling, brush sauce over the meat during the last 10 or 15 minutes of
grilling time. Turn often to prevent burning.   *Bubba Hiers, Albany, GA*

EDDIE'S CHILI

2½ to 3 pounds venison or beef
2   large cans hot chili beans
1   14-ounce bottle catsup
1   large can stewed tomatoes
    Chopped bell pepper
    Chopped onion
    Chopped celery

½   teaspoon chili powder
½   teaspoon cayenne pepper
¼   teaspoon salt
¼   teaspoon black pepper
½   teaspoon Italian seasoning
2 or 3 whole jalapeño peppers

Brown and drain meat. Place in crock pot. Add remaining ingredients.
Cook very slow—at least 3 hours, or overnight if possible. Remove
jalapeño peppers if you prefer, or cut them up and serve with chili.

Eddie Watson, Albany, GA

UNCLE GEORGE'S EGGNOG
This is my Uncle George's favorite eggnog recipe.
This book is dedicated to the memory of Uncle George.

6   eggs, separated
¼   cup plus 6 teaspoons sugar
½   pint whipping cream

½   pint whole milk
½   pint good whiskey
    Ground nutmeg

Beat egg whites until stiff; add ¼ cup of the sugar. Set aside. In another
bowl, add 6 teaspoons sugar to egg yolks; beat until stiff. Whip the
cream until stiff. In a large bowl, combine
ingredients as follows: mix milk into
egg yolks, add egg whites, and stir. Add
whipped cream; fold gently. Fold in
whiskey. Sprinkle cups of cold eggnog
with a small amount of nutmeg.

George Ort III, Atlanta, GA

From my Aunt Peggy's
husband. This self-
made man encouraged,
supported, and
inspired me to finally
open my first
restaurant.

187

PICKLED-EGG SALAD
So easy, you'll never use another recipe.

1 dozen pickled eggs, grated	2 cups mayonnaise
¼ cup finely chopped onion	½ cup Dijon mustard
1 stalk celery, finely chopped	Salt and pepper to taste

Combine all ingredients and mix well. Serve with crusty sourdough bread and pickled watermelon rind. Can be refrigerated for up to three weeks.

Linton Smith, Savannah, GA

VIDALIA ONION PIE

3 cups thinly sliced Vidalia onion	1 teaspoon salt
3 tablespoons butter, melted	2 eggs, beaten
1 9-inch prebaked deep-dish pie shell	3 tablespoons all-purpose flour
½ cup milk	4 slices bacon, crisply cooked and crumbled
1½ cups sour cream	

Preheat oven to 325 degrees. Sauté onion in butter until lightly browned. Spoon into pie shell. Combine milk, sour cream, salt, eggs, and flour. Mix well and pour over onion mixture. Garnish with bacon. Bake for 30 minutes, or until firm in center. Pie has taste and texture of a quiche. Serves 8.

Paul Powell, Washington, DC

Vidalia Onions are Georgia's most famous taste. This sweet onion is grown in Southeast Georgia, just a few miles west of Savannah. The special sweet taste comes from growing the onion seedlings in the mild climate and unique soil within twenty counties, including Toombs County, where Vidalia is located. The growing areas are legally designated by the Georgia Department of Agriculture, and the Vidalia name to describe the onion is a registered certification mark. The first sweet onion was grown on a farm near Vidalia in 1931. Vidalia Onions now represent a $50 million industry, and the onions are available fresh from the fields in late spring and from controlled-atmosphere storage through the fall. They can be stored in a cool dry place to use throughout the year.

We were on the field together at Albany High. I was a cheerleader, and Paul was in the marching band.

HERB CORNBREAD

1¼ cups self-rising cornmeal	¼ teaspoon celery seed
¾ cup self-rising flour	2 eggs, beaten
1 teaspoon sugar	1¼ cups milk
½ teaspoon dried marjoram	6 tablespoons butter,
½ teaspoon dried thyme	melted

Preheat oven to 425 degrees. Combine dry ingredients in a large bowl. Combine eggs, milk, and butter. Add to dry ingredients, stirring until just moistened. Pour batter into a lightly greased 9-inch square pan. Bake for 25 minutes, or until golden brown. Serves 9. *Paul Powell, Washington, DC*

TOM'S SAVANNAH RED RICE

Tom is a dear family friend much loved by the Deen family. In fact, Jennifer and my son Jamie requested that he preside at their marriage. This event consisted of a Methodist bride and a Baptist groom being married by a judge in a Catholic church.

1 cup chopped onion	1 tablespoon Texas Pete or red hot sauce
1 cup chopped bell pepper	1 cup tomato sauce
2 tablespoons butter	1 cup water
1 cup diced Hillshire Farms sausage	3 chicken bouillon cubes
1 14½-ounce can crushed tomatoes with juice	Pepper to taste; add salt to taste if desired
	1 cup uncooked white rice

Preheat oven to 350 degrees. In a saucepan over medium heat, sauté onion and bell pepper in butter. Add sausage; heat until mixture is slightly browned. Add tomatoes, hot sauce, tomato sauce, water, and bouillon cubes. Season with pepper and salt as needed. Stir in rice. Pour mixture into a greased casserole and bake for 45 minutes.
The Honorable Judge Tom Edenfield, Savannah, GA

✔ On March 6, 2004, Judge Edenfield married Michael and me at Bethesda Chapel in Savannah, Georgia.

189

BASIL GRILLED CHICKEN

¾ teaspoon coarsely ground
black pepper
4 skinless chicken breast halves
¼ cup chopped fresh basil, plus 2
tablespoons minced fresh basil
⅓ cup butter, melted, plus ½ cup,
at room temperature

1 tablespoon grated
Parmesan cheese
¼ teaspoon garlic powder
⅛ teaspoon salt
⅛ teaspoon pepper
Fresh basil sprigs,
for garnish (optional)

Prepare fire in a charcoal grill. Press coarsely ground pepper into meaty side of chicken breast halves. Stir chopped basil into melted butter. Brush chicken lightly with butter mixture. In a small bowl, combine softened butter, minced basil, Parmesan cheese, garlic powder, salt, and pepper. Beat at low speed with an electric mixer until smoothly blended. Transfer to a small serving bowl; set aside. Grill chicken over medium coals for 8 to 10 minutes on each side, basting frequently with remaining melted butter mixture. Serve grilled chicken with basil-butter mixture. Garnish with fresh basil sprigs, if desired. *Paul Powell, Washington, DC*

SMOKED GROUPER

1 pound fresh grouper fillet
6 hard-boiled eggs, yolks
removed and reserved
½ cup minced onion
⅓ cup minced red bell pepper
½ cup minced celery
2 tablespoons hot mustard

1 tablespoon mayonnaise
1 tablespoon pickle relish
¼ cup chopped roasted pecans
4 teaspoons caviar, for garnish
4 teaspoons cream cheese,
for garnish
Capers, for garnish

Smoke grouper over mesquite chips. Cut fish into 4 equal pieces. Let cool to room temperature. Mix remaining ingredients, except caviar, cream cheese, and capers. Put mixture into cake decorator or plastic bag with corner cut out. Squeeze equal portions onto fillets. Be creative in your design. Garnish with caviar, cream cheese, and capers. Serve cold. Serves 4. *Tim Oliver, Tybee Island, GA*

FILET MIGNON

1	8-ounce bottle zesty Italian salad dressing	2	slices bacon
2	beef tenderloin fillets, 1½ to 2 inches thick	2	tablespoons Lea and Perrins Steak Sauce
		2	teaspoons water

Pour salad dressing into a shallow pan, place steaks in pan, and let marinate for 3 to 4 hours. Prepare fire in a charcoal grill. Wrap bacon strip around each steak, securing with a toothpick. Grill steaks over hot coals for about 8 minutes per side (5 minutes per side for rare). Baste with mixture of steak sauce and water. For perfect steaks, turn only once.

CLARK'S RED PEPPER SOUP

1	medium onion, chopped	2	tablespoons chopped fresh thyme
2	tablespoons butter		Salt and pepper to taste
4	cloves garlic, minced	½	cup white wine
2	large red bell peppers, roasted and chopped	2	cups chicken stock
		1	cup heavy cream

Over medium heat, sauté onion in butter until soft. Add garlic, red pepper, thyme, salt, and pepper. Add wine and scald. Lower heat and add chicken stock and cream. Cook 3 to 5 minutes and remove from heat. Put in blender and blend until smooth. Return to saucepan and cook for 5 minutes over medium heat. Serve immediately. *Clark Smith, Savannah, GA*

MASHED POTATOES AND SAUTÉED MUSHROOMS

1	stick butter	1	cup white wine
1	cup sliced fresh mushrooms	6	cups (about 2 pounds) diced new potatoes
½	cup diced onion		
2	tablespoons chopped fresh chives	½	cup sour cream
1	clove garlic, chopped		Small amount whole milk

In a saucepan, melt butter and sauté mushrooms, onion, chives, and garlic. Add wine and simmer for about 15 minutes. In a pot, boil potatoes until done; drain. Combine all ingredients and mix. Whip until thick and creamy. Add milk for desired consistency. *Kevin Crumbley, Savannah, GA*

AUTHENTIC ITALIAN ROASTED RED PEPPERS

4	large red bell peppers	2	teaspoons salt, or to taste
1	cup olive oil		Pinch of sugar
2 to 3	cloves garlic, minced		Ground black pepper to taste
1	tablespoon dried basil, or ½ bunch fresh snipped, cleaned basil		

Preheat oven to 450 degrees. Wash red bell peppers and bake until skin is charred; turn periodically to ensure that the skin blackens on all sides. Remove peppers from oven and put into a paper sack. Fold the top of the sack over. Allow peppers to steam in the sack for 30 minutes to 1 hour. Peel the skin from the peppers; pull the peppers into strips, allowing the juice to drip into the bowl where the peppers will go.

Toss the peppers with olive oil, minced garlic, basil, salt, sugar, and pepper. Let stand for several hours. Serve peppers on slices of Italian bread or as a side dish.

George Ort III, Atlanta, GA

Have to say, this apple did not fall far from his father's tree.

BUSTER'S FAMOUS MUSHROOMS

1½	pounds fresh mushrooms, sliced lengthwise		Jane's Krazy Mixed-Up Salt
1	stick butter	¼	cup Worcestershire sauce
		¼	cup water

In large skillet, sauté sliced mushrooms in butter until brown. Sprinkle liberally with Krazy salt. Add Worcestershire sauce and simmer until almost all sauce is absorbed by mushrooms. Add water and continue to simmer until mushrooms are tender. Great with steak or roast beef.

Bill Schumann, Savannah, GA

NOT-TO-BE-TAKEN-SERIOUS TURKEY STUFFING

4	eggs	½	cup chopped celery
4	cups bread crumbs	1	package dry onion soup mix
1	cup uncooked popcorn	1	10- to 20-pound turkey

Beat eggs; add all remaining ingredients except the turkey. Stuff turkey and roast at 375 degrees. When 3 hours are over, get out of the kitchen, because that popcorn stuffing is going to blow that turkey's butt right through the oven door. SUBMITTED FOR FUN ONLY—DO NOT TRY THIS.

ELEPHANT STEW

1	large elephant	2	rabbits
	Salt and pepper to taste		

Take one large elephant and cut into bite-size pieces. Salt and pepper the meat. Place in a large stew pot over outdoor fire. Simmer for about 4 weeks, until tender. This will serve about 4,000 people. If more people come than expected, add the 2 rabbits. But don't do this unless really necessary, because most people don't like to find a hare in their stew.
Paul Powell, Washington, DC

Y'all remember at the beginning of this cookbook I said cooking should be fun? These recipes are just for laughs!

193

INDEX

Appetizers & Beverages

Breads

Candies & Cookies

Candies & Cookies, Continued

Chefs d'Jour

Desserts

Desserts, Continued

Desserts, Continued

Desserts, Continued

Main Dishes & Seafood

Main Dishes & Seafood, Continued

Main Dishes & Seafood, Continued

Salads & Salad Dressings

Vegetables

PAULA DEEN®

Our Family

Paula Deen's FAMILY KITCHEN

PAULA DEEN® STORE

Paula Deen's CREEK HOUSE SEAFOOD & GRILL

the Lady & Sons

PDV — PAULA DEEN VENTURES

DEEN BROTHERS

PAULA DEEN® FOODS

PositivelyPaula

the bag lady foundation

cooking with Paula DEEN

Paula Deen's the bag lady SANDWICHES · SALADS · SWEETS

PAULA DEEN Home

PAULA DEEN Hugs

Visit PAULADEEN.COM